AN OUTLINE OF MODERN HISTORY

THE MACMILLAN COMPAN

NEW YORK · BOSTON · CHICAGO
DALLAS · ATLANTA · SAN FRANCISCO

MACMILLAN & CO., Limited

LONDON · BOMBAY · CALCUTTA
MELBOURNE

THE MACMILLAN CO. OF CANADA, Ltd.

TORONTO

AN OUTLINE OF MODERN HISTORY

A SYLLABUS WITH MAP STUDIES

BY

EDWARD MEAD EARLE, M.A.

LECTURER IN HISTORY, COLUMBIA UNIVERSITY

(Intended to accompany Carlton J. H. HAYES
A Political and Social History of Modern Europe, 2 Volumes.)

New York
THE MACMILLAN COMPANY
1923

COPYRIGHT, 1921,
BY THE MACMILLAN COMPANY.

Set up and electrotyped. Published July, 1921.

INTRODUCTION

This syllabus represents a modest attempt to provide teachers and students with a guide to the study of modern history. The book has been so arranged as to permit of considerable elasticity in its use; it is intended to be suggestive rather than authoritative. The topical outline is planned to be neither too abbreviated to provide a comprehensive basis for study nor so elaborate as to furnish the student with a substitute for careful note-taking. It is believed that the syllabus will offer to teachers a useful plan for collegiate courses in history, without infringing upon the individual's ideas of the relative importance of different parts of the work. Therefore, the topical outline has not been divided into lessons or assignments; no list of books for review or of topics for essays has been appended; no hard and fast rules have been laid down for the map studies. To students—particularly that rapidly growing number who study at home—it is hoped that the syllabus will prove valuable as an aid in the evaluation and co-ordination of facts, as well as in providing a general plan of study.

The course of study here outlined is in very large part the outgrowth of a syllabus used with great success in a beginning course in modern history in Columbia University. This book, indeed, is a complete revision and enlargement of a third edition of that earlier syllabus, published by Columbia University in 1916. The author feels, therefore, that any success he may have had with the present book is due in large measure to the pioneer work of Professors Carlton J. H. Hayes, Austin P. Evans, and Parker Thomas Moon. To Professor Hayes, in particular, he feels deeply grateful for material assistance in the preparation of the work and for a critical reading of the manuscript. Also he is especially indebted to his wife, Beatrice Lowndes Earle, for many helpful suggestions and for corrections in the proof.

EDWARD MEAD EARLE.

Columbia University,
    June 1, 1921

CONTENTS

vii

CONTENTS

BIBLIOGRAPHICAL NOTE

No attempt has been made to append to each section in the topical outline a list of collateral readings. This has appeared to be unnecessary, inasmuch as the text-book upon which this syllabus is based has splendid critical bibliographies at the close of each chapter. From these the instructor or the student may select definite collateral readings containing more detailed accounts of particular subjects than are afforded by the text-book itself. In some instances, however, where it has appeared advisable to suggest additional material for discussion, references are made to other college text-books.

A list of the principal books referred to in the syllabus, and of the abbreviations by which they will be cited, follows:

Text-book Material.

Hayes, C. J. H., *A Political and Social History of Modern Europe,* 2 volumes (New York, The Macmillan Company, 1916). Volume I cited as **Hayes I**; volume II cited as **Hayes II**.

Hayes, C. J. H., *A Brief History of the Great War* (New York, The Macmillan Company, 1920). Cited as **Hayes III**.

Suggested Books for Collateral Readings.

Bassett, J. S., *A Short History of the United States* (New York, The Macmillan Company, 1914). Cited as **Bassett**.

Cheyney, E. P., *An Introduction to the Industrial and Social History of England.* Revised Edition (New York, The Macmillan Company, 1920). Cited as **Cheyney**.

Cross, A. L., *A Shorter History of England and Greater Britain* (New York, The Macmillan Company, 1920). Cited as **Cross**.

Day, Clive, *A History of Commerce* (New York, Longmans, Green & Company, 1919). Cited as **Day**.

Ogg, F. A., *The Governments of Europe.* Revised Edition (New York, The Macmillan Company, 1920.) Cited as **Ogg**.

Atlas Material.

Shepherd, W. R., *Historical Atlas* (New York, Henry Holt & Company, 1911). Cited as **Shepherd.**

Muir, Ramsay, *Hammond's New Historical Atlas for Students.* Fourth Edition. (New York, C. S. Hammond & Company, 1920.) Cited as **Muir.**

Robertson, C. G., and Bartholomew, J. G., *An Historical Atlas of Modern Europe from 1789 to 1914* (New York, The Oxford University Press, 1915). Cited as **Robertson.**

In studying Book VI of the Syllabus, *The Great War,* the student will find it not only advisable, but almost imperative, to supplement the indicated readings with constant references to contemporary periodicals, manuals, and similar publications. As a guide in linking current news with modern history, the student should consult the bibliographical note on pp. 724-725 of **Hayes II,** and a similar bibliography on pp. 431-436 of **Hayes III.** Such "laboratory work" will be of inestimable value in training the student in the methods of historical research and in the critical evaluation of material.

An Outline of Modern History

Book I

FOUNDATIONS OF MODERN EUROPE: EUROPEAN SOCIETY IN THE SIXTEENTH CENTURY

I. The Countries at the Opening of the Century.

A. The new national states.
1. Important factors in the development of each of the national states.
   Territorial and administrative consolidation of the realm.
   Increase of the royal power through
   Suppression of disruptive forces of feudalism.
   Support of the monarch by the middle class.
   Development of an independent revenue by the crown.
   Decrease in the importance of representative assemblies.
2. The national monarchies at the opening of the century.
   Hayes, I, 3-10; Atlas: **Muir,** 8, 15b, 18d.

B. The old Holy Roman Empire.
1. Contrast between the idea of empire and the idea of national monarchy.
2. Territorial extent of the Empire: the Germanies.
3. Government of the Empire: the Emperor; the Electors; the Diet.
4. Vain attempts to achieve national unity; paper reforms of the Diet of Worms (1495).
   Hayes, I, 10-14; Atlas: **Muir,** 23b.

C. The city states.
1. Of Germany.
2. Of Italy.
   Political disunion in Italy and its causes.
   Political and geographical divisions of Italy.

I

3. Of the Netherlands.
>   Hayes, I, 14-20; Atlas: **Muir,** 17c, 20c.

D. Countries of northern and eastern Europe.
1. The Scandinavian states.
2. Grand-duchy of Muscovy (Russia).
3. Feudal states of Poland (including Lithuania) and Hungary.
4. The Sultanate of Turkey (Ottoman Empire).
>   Hayes, I, 20-23; Atlas: **Muir,** 8, 25b, 27.
>   *Map Study Number One* (see p. 129 below).

II. Social and Economic Institutions of the Century.

A. Agriculture.
1. Predominance of agriculture over other occupations; rural population greatly in excess of population of the towns.
2. Division of the agricultural population into two classes: the nobility and the peasantry.
>   The proprietors of the land: the landed aristocracy.
>   The workers of the land: the peasantry,—serfs, free tenants, hired laborers, *métayers*.
>   Preëminence of the nobility.
3. Decline of feudalism and serfdom in western Europe.
4. The manor and the "three field" system of agriculture.
5. Life in the country: isolation, self-sufficiency, and conservatism of the rural community.
>   **Hayes, I,** 28-36. **Cheyney,** 31-46, 120-125; Atlas:
>   **Muir,** Fig. XXVI.

B. Commerce and industry before the commercial revolution.
1. Freedom of life in the towns compared with feudal restrictions of the manor.
2. Organization and regulation of commerce and industry: the gilds.
>   The merchant gilds.
>   Membership and organization.
>   Functions: social, protective, regulative.
>   Decline of the merchant gilds.
>   The craft gilds.
>   Membership and organization.

Regulation of the processes of manufacture.
Partial decay of the craft gilds.
3. The nature of town life in the sixteenth century.
4. Revival of trade with the East: commodities; trade routes.
5. Difficulties of European commerce.
6. European trade centers.
   The Italian and other Mediterranean cities.
   The German towns of the Hanseatic League.
   The Flemish towns of the Netherlands.
      Hayes, I, 36-49; **Cheyney,** 50-62, 68-81, 126-138;
      Day, 79-99; Atlas: **Muir,** 46, 59, 60, Figs.
      XXVII, XXVIII.

C. The commercial revolution.
   1. The age of exploration and discovery.
      Growth of geographical and maritime knowledge.
      Economic and religious motives of the Portuguese and
         Spaniards in the search for new trade routes to the
         East.
      Achievements of the Portuguese, inspired by Prince
         Henry the Navigator: the successful voyage to
         India of Vasco da Gama (1497-1498).
      Achievements of the Spaniards: the voyages of Colum-
         bus; circumnavigation of the earth by Magellan's
         ship (1519-1522).
      Discovery and exploration of America an incident in
         the search for new routes to "the Indies."
   2. The nature of the commercial revolution.
      The discovery of the new routes to the East.
      The importance and necessity of the new routes empha-
         sized by the advance of the Ottoman Turks and the
         partial closing of the old routes.
      The expansion of European commerce to include the
         whole world.
   3. The establishment of colonial empires.
      Early Portuguese, Spanish, and Dutch colonization.
      Beginnings of English and French explorations.
      Motives for colonization: religious and economic.
   4. Effects of the commercial revolution.
      Decline of the Hanseatic and Italian city states and
         increasing importance of the nations of the Atlantic
         seaboard.

Nationalism in commerce: the politico-economic doctrine
of mercantilism.

Development of business organization: commercial companies,—chartered, "regulated," joint-stock; banking.

New commodities of trade. The slave trade.

Expansion of industry and agriculture.

5. General significance of the commercial revolution.

Hayes, I, 27-28, 49-69; **Cheyney,** 138-145; **Day,** 72-
73, 124-137; **Bassett,** 23-44; Atlas: **Muir,** 47, 48.
Map Study Number Two.

III. Political Events of the Century.

A. The career of the Emperor Charles V (1516-1558).
  1. Extent of the Habsburg dominions.
  2. The wars of Charles V and Francis I (1515-1547).
    Causes of the wars. The idea of a "balance of power."
    French efforts in Italy terminated by the Peace of
    Cambrai (1529).
    French expansion toward the Rhine: the treaty of
    Cateau-Cambresis (1559).
  3. Wars with the Turks: attempts to retard the advance of
    Suleiman the Magnificent (1520-1566).
  4. Charles V as Holy Roman Emperor (1519-1558).
    German national patriotism and the aspiration for
    national unity.
    Determination of Charles to strengthen monarchical
    power, but not on a national basis.
    Failure of German nationalism in the sixteenth century.
    The rise of Protestantism.
  5. Relations with England: Henry VIII (1509-1547) and
    Mary Tudor (1553-1558).
  6. Abdication of Charles V and the division of the Habs-
    burg inheritance.

Hayes, I, 74-87, 107; Atlas: **Muir, 8.**

B. The power of Philip II (1556-1598) and its decline.
  1. The policies of Philip II: political, economic, and reli-
    gious,—at home and abroad.
  2. The revolt of the Netherlands (1566-1648).
    Causes: economic, political, religious, personal.
    Spread of the revolt in spite of repressive measures of

the Duke of Alva (1567-1573). William of Orange
as leader of Dutch resistance.
The Pacification of Ghent (1576).
Farnese and the separation of Dutch and Belgian Netherlands: Treaty of Arras and the Union of Utrecht
(1579).
Formal declaration of Dutch independence (1581);
recognition not achieved until peace of Westphalia
(1648).
3. Interference in English affairs.
Failure of intrigue centering in person of Mary Stuart.
Final political and economic triumph of Elizabeth: the
defeat of the Armada (1588) a death-blow to Spanish
naval and commercial supremacy.
4. Interference in French affairs: the War of the Three
Henries.
5. League against the Turks; Ottoman sea power crushed
at Lepanto (1571).
Hayes, I, 87-109; Atlas: Muir, 20a.
Map Study Number Three.

IV. The Religious Revolution of the Century.

A. The Catholic Church at the opening of the century.
1. Peculiarities of religious organizations in 1500 as compared with the present: universal membership, universal
financial support, universal obedience enforced by the
power of the state.
2. Organization of the Catholic Church.
The hierarchy of the pope and the secular clergy.
The regular clergy.
General Church councils.
Relationship between the councils and the pope in
formulation of the canon law, promulgation of
decrees defining dogma, and establishment of ecclesiastical discipline. The "conciliar movement."
3. The nature of the claims and prerogatives of the papacy.
Religious and ecclesiastical.
Temporal and secular.
4. The faith and dogmas of the Catholic Church.
Purpose of the Church: the salvation of souls for
eternity.

Theology.

The sacramental system, "the very center of Catholic theology."

5. Political opposition to the Church.

The claims of the national monarchies incompatible with the claims of the Church and the clergy.

Sources of conflict between church and state.

Ecclesiastical appointments.

Taxation of the clergy and of Church property.

Jurisdiction of ecclesiastical courts.

Extent of the pope's right to intervene in secular affairs.

Royal restrictions on the power of the Church.

6. Religious opposition to the Church.

The Schism between the Catholic Church of the West and the Orthodox Church of the East.

Non-Christian faiths: Mohammedanism and Judaism.

Christian heresies and their extirpation.

Skeptics.

Hayes, I, 112-124.

B. The Protestant revolt and the establishment of national Churches.

1. The general nature of the Protestant revolt: a religious and political movement.

2. The causes of the Protestant revolt.

Political.

Lay opposition to the secular power of the Church.

National monarchy and national patriotism as opposed to international theocracy and cosmopolitan religion.

Economic.

The wealth of the Church.

Ecclesiastical taxes.

Financial abuses in ecclesiastical administration.

Religious.

Abuses in the Church.

Immorality, worldliness, and extravagances of individual popes and lesser clergymen.

Humanist attacks on these abuses.

The rise of a new theology.

Hayes, I, 124-130.

3. Lutheranism: the Protestant revolt in Germany and
Scandinavia.

Martin Luther (1483-1546): his early life and training.

Luther's heretical theology.

Justification by faith.

The Ninety-five Theses (1517) an attack on indul-
gences.

Disputation at Leipzig: separation of Luther from
the Church.

Excommunication of Luther.

Lutheranism in the Germanies.

The Peasants' Revolt (1524-1525).

Peasant grievances and effect of Luther's preaching.

The demands of the peasants: The Twelve Articles.

Luther's denunciation of the peasants' uprising.

Spread of Lutheranism among the princes; the religious wars.

The religious Peace of Augsburg (1555): Provisions,
importance, defects.

Lutheranism in the Scandinavian countries.

Hayes, I, 130-139.

4. Calvinism: the Protestant revolt in Switzerland, France,
Holland, Scotland.

Zwingli (1484-1531) the forerunner of Calvinism in
Switzerland.

John Calvin (1509-1564) and the establishment of
Protestantism in Switzerland.

Calvin's early life and training.

The Institutes of the Christian Religion (1536).

Calvin's régime at Geneva (1536-1564).

The diffusion of Calvinism.

Huguenotism in France.

Middle class nature of French Protestantism.

Nationalism in support of Catholicism.

The Edict of Nantes (1598) and religious toleration.

John Knox and Presbyterianism in Scotland.

The Reformed Churches in the Netherlands and
Germany.

Calvinist sects in England.

Hayes, I, 139-148.

8   AN OUTLINE OF MODERN HISTORY

5. Anglicanism: the Protestant revolt in England.
> Elements of hostility to the Catholic Church in England about 1525.
>> Religious.
>> Political.
>> Personal: the marital difficulties of Henry VIII.
>
> The break with the Catholic Church under Henry VIII.
>> Anti-ecclesiastical measures of 1531 and the excommunication of the King.
>> The Act of Supremacy, 1534.
>> The Six Articles, 1539: reaffirmation of Catholic dogma and faith.
>> Henry's "middle of the road" policy.
>
> Church of England becomes Protestant under Edward VI (1547-1553).
>
> Temporary reversion to Catholicism under Mary Tudor (1553-1558).
>
> Definite fashioning of Anglicanism: the reign of Elizabeth (1558-1603).
>
> English dissent from Anglicanism.
>> **Hayes, I,** 148-156.

C. The Catholic reformation.
1. Catholic complaints against abuses in the Church.
2. Nature of the Catholic reformation.
> Removal of abuses under the reforming popes.
> The Council of Trent (1545-1563).
>> Dogmatic canons: no compromise with Protestantism.
>> Reformatory canons: condemnation and prohibition of abuses.
>
> Consolidation of reforms of the Council of Trent and the enforcement of ecclesiastical discipline: Index and Inquisition.
3. Catholic missionary zeal: Ignatius Loyola and the Jesuits.
4. Political and economic factors in the Catholic reformation.
> **Hayes, I,** 156-164.

D. Summary of the religious revolution of the sixteenth century.
1. Achievement of the Protestant revolt and the Catholic reformation by 1570.
2. Geographical extent of the Protestant revolt.
3. Recapitulation of doctrinal differences.
> Doctrines held in common by Catholics and Protestants.

Doctrines held by all Protestants apart from Catholics.
Divisions among Protestants.
4. General significance of the religious revolution.
Hayes, I, 164-169; Atlas: **Muir,** Figs. IV, V, XIV.

V. The Culture of the Sixteenth Century.

A. Heritage from the past.
    1. From the Greeks and Romans.
    2. From the Mohammedans.
    3. From the mediæval Christians.
       The universities the centers of intellectual life.
       Curricula of the mediæval universities.
       Beginnings of the vernacular languages.
       Gothic architecture.
       Hayes, I, 175-177.

B. The invention of printing and the diffusion of knowledge.
    1. Essential elements in the perfection of printing.
       Development of paper.
       Development of movable type.
    2. Results of the invention of printing.
       Increase in the supply of books.
       Greater degree of accuracy as compared with manual
       copying.
       Diffusion of knowledge and the broadening of education.
       Hayes, I, 177-180.

C. Humanism.
    1. Petrarch (1304-1374), "the father of humanism."
    2. Definition of humanism.
    3. Humanism in the sixteenth century.
       Toleration and encouragement of humanism by the
       Catholic Church.
       Spread of humanism.
       Erasmus (1466-1536), foremost humanist of the century.
       Humanism and Protestantism.
    4. Decline of humanism.
       Hayes, I, 180-185.

D. Art: architecture, sculpture, and painting.
    1. General nature of artistic development: the adaptation of
       classical art-forms to Christian uses.
    2. Sixteenth century the basis of modern artistic life.

3. Great artists of Italy, Germany, the Netherlands, and Spain.
   Hayes, I, 185-192.

E. Development of music and musical instruments.
    Hayes, I, 192.

F. The national literatures.
    1. Latin the universal language of culture in the middle ages.
    2. Gradual spread of the vernacular languages.
    3. National literatures of the sixteenth century a result of complex social developments.
    4. Literature and authors in Italy, France, Spain, Portugal, Germany, England.
       Hayes, I, 193-196.

G. Beginnings of modern natural science.
    1. Scientific characteristics of the century.
       Humanism,—the spirit of criticism and the expansion of intellectual interests.
       The invention of printing.
       Maritime discovery and the expansion of geographical knowledge.
       The development of the sciences and of scientific method.
    2. Development and popularization of the science of astronomy.
       Limitations of mediæval astronomical knowledge.
       Ignorance and superstition: horoscopes and astrology.
       The Ptolemaic System.
       Copernicus (1473-1543) and his theory of the solar system.
       The Copernican System developed and popularized: Kepler (1571-1630) and Galileo (1564-1642).
    3. Effective beginnings of modern scientific method.
       Deductive reasoning the prevalent scientific method of ancient and mediæval scholars; its limitations and defects.
       Francis Bacon (1561-1626): emphasis upon the necessity of inductive reasoning in scientific advance.
       Descartes (1596-1660): emphasis upon observation and experiment in the collection of facts.
       Hayes, I, 196-201.

Book II

DYNASTIC AND COLONIAL RIVALRY

PART I. THE GROWTH OF ABSOLUTISM IN FRANCE AND THE STRUGGLE BETWEEN BOURBONS AND HABSBURGS IN THE SEVENTEENTH AND EIGHTEENTH CENTURIES

I. Growth of Absolutism in France under Henry IV, Richelieu, and Mazarin.

A. Introductory: review of French affairs in the sixteenth century.
1. Political: the nobles and the Protestants threaten the royal power.
2. Religious.
    Wars between Guises and Bourbons; Catherine de Medici and the policy of "trimming."
    Qualified religious toleration: the Edict of Nantes (1598).
3. Economic.
    Waste and ruin attendant upon the protracted civil and religious wars.
    Bankruptcy of the national treasury.

B. The reign of Henry IV (1589-1610).
1. Economic reorganization: the reforms of Sully.
    Retrenchment and efficiency in government finance.
    Agricultural development.
2. Economic reorganization: encouragement of the middle class.
    Foundations of the silk industry.
    Colonial and commercial development.
3. Foreign affairs: the "Grand Design."

C. The regency of Marie de Medici (1610-1624).
1. Extravagance and unpopularity of Marie de Medici.
2. Futile meeting of the Estates General (1614).

11

D. Richelieu (1624-1642) and the triumph of absolutism.
    1. Two-fold aim of Richelieu's policies.
        Supremacy of the royal power in France.
        Predominance of France in European affairs.
    2. The achievement of absolutism.
        Disappearance of representative government.
        Reorganization of the royal army.
        Removal of political privileges of the Huguenots.
        Repression of the nobles.
        Administrative centralization: the *intendants*.
    3. Significance of the régime of Richelieu.

E. Mazarin (1642-1661) and consolidation of the work of Richelieu.
    1. The Fronde (1648-1653).
    2. Results of the Fronde.
        The nobility discredited.
        Financial and political privileges of the parlements revoked.
        Paris disarmed and deprived of local self-government.
        The last attempt before the Revolution to cast off royal absolutism.
        Hayes, I, 209-218.

II. The Thirty Years' War (1618-1648).

A. The dynastic character of wars in the seventeenth century: rivalry of the Habsburgs and the Bourbons.

B. Religious and political antecedents of the War in the Germanies.
    1. Weaknesses of the Peace of Augsburg.
    2. The union of Protestant princes and the Catholic League of Princes.
    3. Particularism and jealousies of the German princes.
    4. Foreign allies of the princes.

C. The four periods of the War.
    1. The Bohemian Revolt (1618-1620).
    2. The Danish period (1625-1629).
    3. The Swedish period (1630-1635).
        Causes: the policies and ambition of Gustavus Adolphus (1611-1632).
        The occasion: the imperial Edict of Restitution (1629).
        The allies of Sweden.

Generalship of Gustavus Adolphus.

Defeat and death of Tilly (April, 1632).

Defeat of Wallenstein (November, 1632); Gustavus Adolphus killed.

Treaty of Prague (1635).

4. The French, or international, period (1635-1648).

Richelieu's motives: the War as a phase of the rivalry of Bourbons and Habsburgs.

French military supremacy: Condé and Turenne.

D. The Peace of Westphalia (1648).
1. Political provisions.
2. Religious provisions: permanence of the religious settlement.
3. Significance of the treaties of Westphalia in Germany.
4. Humiliation of the Habsburgs and increased prestige of the Bourbons.

E. Economic ruin of Germany a result of the protracted struggle.

F. The Peace of the Pyrenees (1659); termination of the struggle between France and Spain.

G. The Thirty Years' War and international law.
1. The origins and development of international law and diplomacy.
2. Influence of the Thirty Years' War on international law.
The theory of independent sovereign states vs. the theory of Empire.
The brutality of the War: the need for protection of non-combatants, sick, and wounded.
3. Hugo Grotius; first systematic treatise on international law, *On the Law of War and Peace.*
Hayes, I, 218-232. Atlas: **Muir,** 9, Fig. XX.

III.   The Age of Louis XIV.

A. Absolutism during the reign of Louis XIV (1643-1715).
1. The ministry of Mazarin terminated (1661) by death; personal rule of the King (1661-1715).
2. Louis XIV the heir to absolutist tendencies.
3. Bossuet and the theory of monarchy by "Divine Right."
4. Louis XIV the foremost personification of Bossuet's theory: "The Age of Louis XIV."

B. The government of France.
  1. Administration: "rule of the robe."
  2. Economic reform: the ministry of Colbert.
    Colbert (1619-1683): his career and middle class point of view.
    Attempted financial reform.
    Encouragement of agriculture, industry, and commerce.
    French mercantilism under Colbert.
    Colbert's "world policy."
  3. Militarism: military reorganization under Louvois and Vauban.
  4. Splendor and glamour of the government deceptive of the true economic condition of the country.

C. Religious policies of Louis XIV.
  1. Persecution of the Protestants and revocation of the Edict of Nantes (1685).
    Hayes, I, 235-242.

D. Foreign policies of Louis XIV: extension of French frontiers.
  1. Traditional French policy of opposition to the Habsburgs.
  2. The doctrine of "natural boundaries."
  3. Habsburg territories coveted by France.

E. The wars of Louis XIV.
  1. The War of Devolution (1667-1668).
    Cause: Maria Theresa's "claim" to the Spanish Netherlands.
    Isolation of Spain by diplomacy.
    The Triple Alliance to preserve the "balance of power."
    Treaty of Aix-la-Chapelle (1668).
  2. The Dutch War (1672-1678).
    Franco-Dutch rivalry, political and economic.
    Diplomatic isolation of Holland.
    Internal strife in Holland.
    Invasion of Holland by the French.
    Intervention of the Emperor, the Elector of Brandenburg, and Spain. Threatened English intervention.
    Treaty of Nijmwegen (1678).
    Effects of the Dutch War on France.
  3. War of the League of Augsburg, or of the Palatinate (1689-1697).
    Causes.
    The French "Chambers of Reunion."

French annexations without war.

The League of Augsburg (1686) to resist French
aggression.

French invasion of the Palatinate.

Holland and England, under William III, join the
League of Augsburg.

Beginning of a new Hundred Years' War between
France and England,—dynastic, colonial, commercial.

Treaty of Ryswick (1697).

4. War of the Spanish Succession (1702-1713).

The question of the Spanish succession creates a delicate international situation.

Rival claimants to the inheritance in default of a
male heir to Charles II.

"Balance of power": objection to both claimants.

Commercial and colonial complications.

Will of Charles II: accession of Philip of Anjou.

The Grand Alliance against the Bourbons.

French military reverses: the invasion of France.

The Peace of Utrecht (1713-1714) and its significance.

5. Disastrous effects of wars of Louis XIV upon France.

F. Decline of France.

1. Last years of Louis XIV.

2. Misgovernment during the minority of Louis XV.

Hayes, I, 242-258; Atlas: Muir, 10, 150.

Map Study Number Four.

PART II. THE TRIUMPH OF PARLIAMENTARY GOVERNMENT IN ENGLAND.

I. Conflicting Political Tendencies in England: Absolutism versus Parliamentarianism.

A. Absolutism of the Tudors (1485-1603), a precedent for the
Stuarts.

1. Absolutism achieved earlier in England than in France.

2. Strengthening of the royal power under the Tudors.

3. Signs of opposition to absolutism in the last days of
Elizabeth.

4. Accession of the Stuart Dynasty (1603): absolutism in
theory as well as in practice.

The Stuarts, heirs to the absolutist practice of the Tudors.

James I (1603-1625) and the Stuart theory of divine-right monarchy,—*"a deo rex, a rege lex."*

B. The English tradition of restrictions upon royal power: the evolution of constitutional government.
   1. Magna Carta (1215).
   2. The origins and development of Parliament.
      The House of Lords.
      The House of Commons.
   3. Evolution of the powers of Parliament.

C. Practices of absolutism inconsistent with the tradition of representative government: the struggle between Parliament and James I.
   1. Early controversies between King and Parliament become increasingly bitter.
      Extravagance of the King and parsimony of the Commons: "illegal taxation."
      Attempts of Parliament to control appointments and foreign policy.
   2. Political dispute complicated by religious factors.
      Calvinism in England.
      "Puritans" in the Anglican Church.
      Independents, or Separatists.
      Insistence of the King upon uniformity: the Hampton Court Conference (1604).
      Hatred of the Puritans for James I.
   3. Commercial and religious opposition to foreign policy of the King.
   4. Interconnection of Puritanism, commercialism, and parliamentarianism.

D. Struggle for parliamentary government continued: Charles I (1625-1649).
   1. Character of Charles I; his devotion to absolutism.
   2. Continuation of the conflict between King and Parliament.
      Dissolution of the first and second parliaments.
      The third Parliament and the Petition of Right (1628).
   3. "Personal" rule of Charles I, 1629-1640.
      Taxation without consent of Parliament.
      Miscellaneous devices for procuring a revenue.
      The obnoxious "ship money": trial of John Hampden.

Religious controversies.
Policies of Archbishop Laud.
Enforcement of uniformity.
4. Outbreak of the Scotch revolt (1638) and its success
compel the King to seek aid from Parliament.
The Short Parliament.
Convocation of the Long Parliament (1640).
Hayes, I, 261-274, 294; **Cross,** 264-269, 283-285.

II. The Puritan Revolution.

A. Reforms of the Long Parliament.
1. Impeachment and arrest of Wentworth and Laud.
2. Abolition of special tribunals.
3. Renewed prohibition of illegal taxation.
4. The "Triennial Act."

B. The Great Rebellion (1642-1646).
1. Violation of parliamentary privileges by the King leads
to the passage of laws without his consent and to
the levy of troops against his will.
2. Parties to the Civil War: Cavaliers and Roundheads.
3. Divisions among the revolutionists; predominance of the
Presbyterians in the Long Parliament.
4. Presbyterian phase of the revolt.
"Solemn League and Covenant" with the Scots (1643).
Battle of Marston Moor (1644).
Religious intolerance.
Negotiations for the restoration of the King.
5. The Independents and the "New Model" army: Oliver
Cromwell.

C. The Commonwealth (1649-1660).
1. The "Rump" Parliament and the declaration of the
Commonwealth.
2. Reasons for the success of the oligarchical Commonwealth.
3. Popular and successful foreign policy.
Navigation Act, 1651.
Trade wars with the Dutch.
4. Restoration of order.
Execution of the King (1649).

Ruthless suppression of the Irish rebellion.
Defeat of the Scots.
5. Dissolution of the Rump Parliament by Cromwell (1653).
6. The Protectorate (1653-1659).
Character and career of Oliver Cromwell (1599-1658).
Transition from Commonwealth to Protectorate: "Barebone's Parliament."
The "Instrument of Government."
Parliament under the Protectorate.
Sources of strength and weakness of the Protectorate.
Disorganization following the death of Cromwell: failure of Richard Cromwell.
Hayes, I, 274-281; Atlas: **Muir,** 38, 40a.

III.   The Restoration.

A.   The royalist reaction.
  1. Popular grievances against the Protectorate.
  2. Opposition to Puritanism.

B.   Conditions of the restoration of Charles II (1660-1685).

C.   Renewed constitutional conflict between King and Parliament.
  1. Financial disputes.
Extravagances of the King.
Illicit revenue.
  Treaty of Dover (1670).
  2. Religious disputes.
Parliamentary reaction in favor of Anglicanism.
Royal leanings toward Roman Catholicism: "Declaration of Indulgence" (1672).
Popular fear of Catholicism: the Exclusion Bill (1679).
  3. Party alignments: Whigs and Tories.

D.   The reign of James II (1685-1688).
  1. Alienation of popular sympathy and support: disastrous combination of absolutism and Roman Catholicism.
Hayes, I, 281-287.

IV.   The "Glorious Revolution": the Establishment of Parliamentary Government.

A.   Dethronement of James II (1688) and the accession of William and Mary.

B.   The constitutional settlement.
    1.   The Bill of Rights (1689).
    2.   The Mutiny Act (1689).
    3.   The Act of Settlement (1701).
    4.   The Act of Union with Scotland (1707).

C.   The religious settlement: The Act of Toleration (1689).

D.   Accession of the Hanoverians: the era of Whig domination (1714-1761).
    1.   Continued decline of the royal power under George I (1714-1727) and George II (1727-1760).
    2.   Development of the Cabinet and ministerial responsibility to Parliament.
    3.   The ministry of Robert Walpole (1721-1742).
    4.   Policies of William Pitt, Earl of Chatham.

E.   Summary of English constitutional development in the seventeenth and early eighteenth centuries.
    1.   Repudiation of the theory of monarchy by divine right.
    2.   Supremacy of Parliament and ministers responsible to Parliament.
    3.   Reasons for early development of constitutional government in England.
    4.   English government parliamentary, not democratic.
        "Unreformed" House of Commons.
        Restricted suffrage: the commercial aristocrats.
        House of Lords: the landed aristocrats.
            Hayes, I, 287-293, 295.

PART III.   THE WORLD CONFLICT OF FRANCE AND GREAT BRITAIN

I.   French and English Colonies in the Seventeenth Century. Relative Position of the Rivals in 1688.

A.   Claims and possessions in America.

B.   Early colonial establishments in Africa.

C.   French and English rivalry in India.
    1.   India a field for commerce and trade, not for colonization.
    2.   Disunion and weakness of the Mogul empire.
        Religious causes.
        Geographic and economic causes.

3. Important English possessions in India.
4. French posts in India.

D. Comparative resources of France and England.
> Hayes, I, 299-306; Bassett, 81, 111-115; Atlas: **Muir,** 54a.
> *Map Study Number Five* (Part A).

II.   Preliminary Encounters, 1689-1748.

A. War of the League of Augsburg in its colonial aspects: King William's War (1689-1697).
   1. Indecisive character of the peace of Ryswick.

B. War of the Spanish Succession: Queen Anne's War in America (1702-1713).
   1. Military operations in the American colonies.
   2. Importance of the Peace of Utrecht.
      English gains in America and in the Mediterranean.
      The Asiento.

C. The interlude of peace, 1713-1739.
   1. French aggressiveness in America and in India.
   2. Trade disputes between Spain and Great Britain: the War of Jenkins's Ear (1739).

D. War of the Austrian Succession (1740-1748): King George's War in the colonies (1744-1748).
   1. Indecisive character of the military operations in America.
   2. The struggle in India: Dupleix.
   3. The Treaty of Aix-la-Chapelle.
   > Hayes, I, 306-312; Bassett, 115-120; Atlas: **Muir,** 49a.

III.   The Triumph of Great Britain: The Seven Years' War, 1756-1763.

A. World-wide extent of the Seven Years' War.

B. The war in North America: the French and Indian War (1754-1763).
   1. The struggle for the possession of the Ohio Valley.
   2. English invasion of Canada: Montcalm versus Wolfe.
   3. Futile intervention of Spain.
   4. British successes and the downfall of "New France."

C. The Seven Years' War in India.
   1. The rival leaders: Clive and Dupleix.
   2. French failure in the Carnatic.
   3. Clive's campaign in Bengal: Plassey (1757).
   4. Fall of Pondicherry (1761); collapse of the French dominion in India.

D. Colonial aspects of the Treaty of Paris.
   1. Remnants of the French colonial empire in America and in India.
   2. The settlement with Spain.
   3. Great gains of England.

E. Significance of the Seven Years' War.
   1. Establishment of the British Empire and the spread of the English language and English civilization.
   2. British commercial and maritime supremacy.
   3. Temporary ruin of France,—colonial, commercial, naval, financial.

F. Aftermath of the Seven Years' War: French participation in the War of American Independence.
   Hayes, I, 312-319; **Bassett,** 121-132; Atlas: **Muir,** 50a, 55, 56a, 61a.
   Map Study Number Five (Parts B and C).

PART IV. THE REVOLUTION WITHIN THE BRITISH EMPIRE

I. The British Colonial System in the Eighteenth Century.

A. Mercantilism the keynote of British colonial policy.
   1. Mercantilism in theory and practice.
      Regulation of colonial industry and commerce.
      Taxation.
   2. Early colonial toleration of mercantilist restrictions.
      The policy of "salutary neglect" and other factors.
   3. Altered situation after the French and Indian War: policies of George III.
   4. "Taxation without representation."
      The financial measures of the Grenville ministry.
      The Townshend Acts (1767).
      Increasing colonial resistance.

B. Failure of mercantilism in the American colonies.
   1. The ministry of Lord North.
     Failure of conciliation.
     The "Intolerable Acts" (1774).
   2. Colonial non-importation agreements.
       Hayes, I, 322-331; **Bassett,** 99-101, 140-145, 157-158.
       161-179.

II. The War of American Independence.

A. Outbreak of the revolt of the thirteen colonies.

B. Declaration of Independence (1776).
   1. The colonies as a belligerent nation.
   2. Influence of French philosophical radicals.

C. Grave difficulties of the revolutionists and early British successes.

D. The French alliance and the diplomatic isolation of Great Britain.

E. The War in Europe and America.

F. The defeat of Great Britain.
   1. Treaties of Paris and Versailles (1783).
   2. Settlement between Great Britain and Holland (1784).
       Hayes, I, 332-337; Atlas: **Muir,** 55, 56a.

III. The Reformation of the British Empire.

A. New conciliatory colonial policy.
   1. Political concessions in Canada, India, Ireland.
   2. Economic concessions: decline and gradual abandonment of mercantilism: *laisser-faire*.

B. Extension and solidification of the British Empire.
   1. India: conquests and administrative reforms of Hastings and Cornwallis.
   2. The Straits Settlements and Australia.
       Hayes, I, 337-340.

PART V. THE GERMANIES IN THE EIGHTEENTH CENTURY

I. Deplorable Condition of Germany after the Thirty Years' War.

A. Political: the Holy Roman Empire in decline.
 1. Persistence of the forms of the Empire in spite of declining power and prestige.
 2. Low ebb of national enthusiasm.
 3. Foreign intervention and influence in the affairs of the Empire.
 4. "Sovereignty" and particularism of the princes.

B. Social: moral and intellectual torpor.

C. Economic: paralysis of industry and commerce.
 1. Decline in wealth and influence of the commercial classes: abandonment of the Hanseatic League.
 2. Impoverishment and oppression of the peasantry.
 Hayes, I, 342-344.

II. The Habsburg Dominions.

A. The possessions of Charles VI (1711-1740).

B. Check upon Habsburg ambitions in the Germanies.
 1. Non-German interests and problems a source of weakness to the Habsburgs.
 2. The Habsburgs a source of weakness to the Germanies.
 3. Continued prestige of the Habsburgs in German affairs.

C. Question of the Habsburg inheritance.
 1. The "Pragmatic Sanction" of Charles VI.
 2. Diplomatic negotiations to secure recognition of the Pragmatic Sanction.
 3. Accession of Maria Theresa (1740-1780).
 Hayes, I, 344-347; Atlas: **Muir,** 25a; **Robertson,** 19.

III. The Rise of Prussia.

A. The rising fortunes of the house of Hohenzollern.
 1. Early history and territorial acquisitions.

B. Brandenburg under Frederick William, the Great Elector
   (1640-1688).
   1. Gains of Brandenburg by Peace of Westphalia.
   2. Reforms of the Great Elector.
      Administrative consolidation of the realm: the accom-
         plishment of absolutism.
      Financial retrenchment and economic development.
      Military reorganization.
C. Brandenburg-Prussia a kingdom.
   1. Frederick I, "King in Prussia" (1701).
   2. Benevolent despotism of Frederick William I.
      Further administrative centralization: the "general
         directory."
      Development of military strength and efficiency.
      Financial reform.
      Social and economic development.
   3. Accession of Frederick II (1740).
            Hayes, I, 347-352, 363; Atlas: **Muir,** 24a.
            Map Study Number Six.

IV. The Minor German States.

A. Bavaria.
   1. Religious and international policies of the Wittelsbachs.
B. Saxony.
   1. Strategic geographical position of Saxony.
   2. Prestige of Saxony.
   3. Weaknesses in the position of the Wettin family.
C. Hanover.
            Hayes, I, 352-354.

V. The Struggle between Hohenzollerns and Habsburgs.

A. Comparative resources of the Hohenzollerns and Habsburgs in
   1740.
   1. Relative military and financial strength.
   2. Leadership: Frederick the Great (1740-1786) versus
      Maria Theresa (1740-1780).
B. The War of the Austrian Succession (1740-1748).
   1. The coalition against Maria Theresa.
   2. Outbreak of the war: Prussian occupation of Silesia.

3. The allies of Maria Theresa.
4. Course of the war.
5. Treaties of Aix-la-Chapelle.
6. Significance of the War of the Austrian Succession in German affairs.

C. The Seven Years' War (1756-1763).
   1. Alignment of the powers for the struggle: the "Diplomatic Revolution."
   2. Outbreak of hostilities in Europe: the invasion of Saxony (1756).
   3. Precarious position of Prussia: the brilliant generalship of Frederick.
   4. Withdrawal of Russia from the coalition.
   5. Treaty of Hubertusburg (1763).
   6. Significance of the Seven Years' War in the struggle between Habsburgs and Hohenzollerns.

D. The first partition of Poland (1772).
   1. Acquisitions of Prussia and of Austria.
   2. Effects of the partition upon Prussia and upon Austria.

E. Summary of the conflict between Hohenzollerns and Habsburgs in the eighteenth century.

   Hayes, I, 354-362; Atlas: **Muir,** 10, 24a, 26b; **Robertson,** 11, 19, 27.

PART VI. THE RISE OF RUSSIA AND THE DECLINE OF TURKEY, SWEDEN, AND POLAND

I. Russia in the Seventeenth Century.

A. Contrast between the Russia of the seventeenth century and the Russia of 1914.

B. The expansion of Russia.
   1. Factors in extension of the Russian dominion.
   2. Russian expansion in Europe.
   3. Migration of the Russians into Asia.
   4. Extension of territory and extension of the power of the tsar.

C. Oriental characteristics of Russia.
   1. Religious.

2. Social: contact with the East.
3. Natural obstacles in the way of association with the West.
Predominance of agriculture.
Lack of seaports.

D. The "troublous times" and the accession of the Romanovs.
Hayes, I, 366-369, 389; Atlas: **Muir,** 26, 27.

II. Peter the Great (1682-1725): Decline of Sweden.

A. Accession as sole ruler (1696) and early travels of Peter the Great.

B. Europeanization of Russia: the reforms of Peter the Great.
1. Political: the establishment of absolutism.
Suppression of the *streltsi*.
Reorganization of the army.
Subordination of Church to state: the Holy Synod.
Administrative centralization in the person of the tsar.
2. Social and economic.
Introduction of occidental customs.
Bungling attempts to encourage agriculture, industry, commerce.

C. Foreign policy of Peter the Great.
1. Aims of his policy.
Aggrandizement in the east.
"Windows" to the west.
2. Obstacles in the way of realization: Sweden and Turkey.

D. Russian aggrandizement at the expense of Sweden.
1. Greatness of Sweden in the seventeenth century.
Political: the imperialism of Gustavus Adolphus and his successors.
Religious.
Economic: importance of Sweden in the Baltic trade.
2. Weaknesses of the position of Sweden at the opening of the eighteenth century.
3. Coalition against Charles XII (1697-1718): proposed partition of 1699.
4. Military exploits of the boy king: the Great Northern War (1699-1721).
Poltava (1709) the high water mark of the fortunes of Charles XII.

Death of Charles (1718).

Treaties of Stockholm (1719 and 1720).

Treaty of Nystad (1721): partial achievement of the western policy of Peter the Great.

E. Failure of Peter's attempted expansion at the expense of Turkey.
  Hayes, I, 369-379.

III. Catherine the Great (1762-1796): Defeat of Turkey and Dismemberment of Poland.

A. Reforms of Catherine II: the extension of absolutism.

B. Foreign policy: Russian aggrandizement at the expense of Poland.

 1. The Kingdom of Poland in the eighteenth century: causes of weakness and disunion.
  Geographical.
  Ethnological.
  Religious.
  Social.
  Political.

 2. Early Russian interference in Polish affairs: the election of 1764.

 3. The partition of Poland.
  First partition (1772).
  Second partition (1793).
  Third partition (1795).

C. Foreign policy: Russian aggrandizement at the expense of Turkey.

 1. Decline of Ottoman power in the seventeenth century.

 2. Weaknesses of the Turkish empire.

 3. Catherine's war with the Turks (1768-1774).
  Russian successes.
  Treaty of Kuchuk Kainarji (1774).
  Importance of the treaty.
   Hayes, I, 379-388; Atlas: **Muir,** 26, 27; **Robertson,** 27, 29.

Book III

"LIBERTY, EQUALITY, FRATERNITY"

PART I: EUROPEAN SOCIETY IN THE EIGHTEENTH CENTURY

I. Social and Economic Conditions of the Century.

A. General similarity of sixteenth century and eighteenth century life.

B. Agriculture in the eighteenth century.
    1. Survival of primitive methods.
    2. Beginnings of better agriculture: "gentlemen farmers" and "husbandry."
    3. Persistence of manorial system, with some modifications.
    4. Burden of taxation on the peasantry.
    5. Sorry condition of the peasantry.

C. Commerce and industry in the eighteenth century.
    1. Remarkable development of town life.
    2. General nature of industry in the eighteenth century.
        Production for other than the home market.
        Restrictions on industry.
            Survival of gild regulations.
            Government regulation: mercantilism.
        Mercantilist encouragement of new industries.
    3. Commerce in the eighteenth century.
        Restrictions and handicaps.
            Poor transportation.
            Internal tariffs and customs.
            Mercantilism.
        Remarkable growth of commerce.
    4. Social consequences of the development of industry and commerce.
        Rise of the *bourgeoisie*.

D. Society in the eighteenth century.
    1. The "privileged" classes and their privileges.
    2. Declining usefulness of the privileged classes.
       The higher nobility.
         Feudal services no longer necessary.
         Absentee landlordism.
       The higher clergy.
         Hayes, I, 395-406; **H. de B. Gibbins,** *Industry in England* (New York, 1916), 265-340.

II. Religious and Ecclesiastical Conditions of the Century.

A. The Roman Catholic Church.
    1. Extent.
    2. Organization, faith, and dogmas.
    3. Disappearance of secular privileges in Protestant countries.
    4. Relations between Church and State in Catholic countries.
       Curtailment of papal privileges.
       Surviving privileges of the Church.
    5. Internal dissensions.
       Jansenism.
       Febronianism and Ultramontanism.
       Suppression of the Jesuit order (1773).

B. The Anglican Church.
    1. Privileged position of the Established Church in the British Isles.
    2. Illiberal policy toward Protestant Dissenters and Roman Catholics.
       In England and Scotland.
       In Ireland.
    3. Dissenting Protestant sects in England.
       Presbyterians and Separatists.
       Baptists, Unitarians, Quakers.
       Methodists: significance of the Methodist movement.

C. Protestant churches on the Continent.
    1. The Lutheran churches.
    2. The Reformed churches.
    3. Extent of Protestantism on the Continent.

D. Growth of skepticism and indifference.
    1. Deism and its results.

E. Summary of the religious situation in the eighteenth century.
  1. Nationalism in religion.
    Protestant state churches.
    Nationalism in Catholic countries: "Liberties of the Gallican Church."
  2. Differences of doctrine and organization promote disunity among Protestant sects.
  3. Numbers and influence of the assailants of Christianity.
    Hayes, I, 406-414.

III. Scientific and Intellectual Developments of the Century.

A. Science in the eighteenth century.
  1. The scientific spirit: debt to Bacon and Descartes.
  2. Progress of experimental science.
    The achievements of Sir Isaac Newton in astronomy and physics.
    Experimentation in electricity, chemistry, physiology, medicine.
    Extension of geographical knowledge: scientific exploration.
  3. Popularity of the new science.

B. Philosophy: the spirit of progress and reform in the eighteenth century.
  1. Growing confidence in the powers of the human mind: "rationalism."
  2. Rationalist philosophy.
    Importance of the writings of the Englishman John Locke (1632-1704).
    Rationalism in France.
    The influence of Voltaire (1694-1778).
    Popularization of rationalism: Diderot and the Encyclopedists.
  3. Political philosophy.
    Political theories of John Locke.
    Criticism of political institutions: Montesquieu (1689-1755); Rousseau (1712-1778).
    Criticism of the administration of justice: Beccaria.
  4. Social and economic philosophy.
    Speculations of Rousseau on private property.
    New ideas of education expounded by Rousseau.

Beginnings of the science of political economy.
The Physiocrats and the doctrine of *laisser-faire:*
Quesnay and Turgot.
Adam Smith: *The Wealth of Nations* (1776).
Hayes, I, 414-426

IV. Political Institutions: European Governments of the Eighteenth Century.

A. The British monarchy.
   1. Territories of the British monarchy.
      England (including Wales) and Scotland.
      The royal colonies.
      Ireland.
         Semi-independence of Ireland (1782-1801): the Irish Parliament.
         Act of Union: Irish representation in the Parliament of the United Kingdom.
   2. The king and Parliament.
      Nominal powers of the king.
      Constitutional limitations upon the powers of the king.
      The powers of Parliament.
   3. Undemocratic character of Parliament.
      The aristocratic House of Lords.
      Unrepresentative House of Commons.
         Restricted suffrage.
         Unequal apportionment of representation.
         Corruption in elections.
   4. Parliament and the Cabinet.
      Influence of parliamentary bribery and corruption.
      Development of the cabinet system and the principle of ministerial responsibility.
      The reign of George III: attempted royal control of Parliament and the Cabinet.
   5. Growing demand for reform.
      John Wilkes.
      Charles James Fox and the program of reform.
      William Pitt, the younger (1759-1806), and the "New Tories."
   6. Reaction against reform: effect of the French Revolution upon the upper classes in England.
         Hayes, I, 430-440.

B. The "enlightened despots."
    1. Contrast between English theories of representative, constitutional government and the Continental idea of monarchy by divine right.
    2. The nature of "enlightened despotism."
    3. Typical enlightened despots.
       Frederick the Great of Prussia (1740-1786).
          Frederick's theories of the powers and responsibilities of kingship.
          Reforms of Frederick the Great.
          Frederick's interest in philosophy.
       Catherine the Great of Russia (1762-1796).
       Charles III of Spain.
       Joseph I of Portugal.
       Joseph II of Austria (1780-1790), Holy Roman Emperor (1765-1790).
          Heritage from Maria Theresa.
          Joseph's faith in rationalism.
          Attempted reforms of Joseph II.
          Failure of Joseph II.
    4. Weaknesses of benevolent despotism.
       Hayes, I, 440-448; Atlas: **Robertson, 5.**

C. Unenlightened despotism: the French monarchy.
    1. French people better off than their neighbors,—a cause of French criticism of their political institutions.
    2. The French administrative system.
       The king and his powers.
       The Royal Council.
       Local administration.
    3. Confusion and corruption in the government of France.
       In administration.
       In the laws and the administration of justice.
       In the army.
       In finance.
    4. Growing complaints against the French monarchy under Louis XV (1715-1774).
       The increasing burden of taxation.
       The King as a personification of the dangers of hereditary despotism.
    5. Attempted reforms under Louis XVI (1774-1792).

The ministry and economic policies of Turgot (1774-1776).

Financial policies of Necker (1776-1781).

Opposition of the privileged classes to reform.

6. Failure of absolutism in France.

Effect upon France of participation in the War of American Independence.

The financial crisis and the Assembly of the Notables (1787).

The death-knell of absolutism: convocation of the Estates General.

Hayes, I, 449-461; Atlas: **Robertson, 7.**

Map Study Number Seven (*Part* A).

PART II. THE FRENCH REVOLUTION

I. Introductory: General Nature and Causes of the Revolution.

A. The old régime challenged by new conditions.
  1. Progress and the spirit of reform opposed to outworn institutions.
  2. Conflicting theories in the Revolution.
     Divine right monarchy versus democracy.
     Class distinctions versus social equality.

B. Reasons for the outbreak of revolution in France, rather than elsewhere.

C. Differences between the French and English revolutions.

D. Conflicting class interests in the Revolution.
     Hayes, I, 464-468.

II. The End of Absolutism in France.

A. Financial difficulties of Louis XVI; convocation of the Estates General.

B. The Estates General.
  1. Character of the institution.
  2. Temper of the delegates: the *cahiers.*
  3. Influence of the Third Estate and its leaders: Mirabeau and Sieyès.
  4. The constitutional question of organization.

C. Transformation of the Estates General into the National Constituent Assembly.
  1. "Oath of the Tennis Court," June 20, 1789.
  2. Popular demonstrations in support of the Assembly.
    Destruction of the Bastille, July 14, 1789.
    The Paris Commune.
    "March of the Women to Versailles," October 5, 1789.
    Forcible removal of the government to Paris.
  3. Beginnings of the social revolution.
      Hayes, I, 468-479; Atlas: **Muir,** 15e.

III. The End of the Old Régime: Achievements of the National Constituent Assembly, 1789-1791.

A. Social equalization: "The August Days."
  1. Legal destruction of feudalism and serfdom.
  2. Abolition of privilege.
  3. Causes of legislation of "The August Days."
  4. Importance of "the decree abolishing the feudal system."

B. The Declaration of the Rights of Man.

C. Reform of local administration: the departments.

D. Regulation of the national finances.
  1. Tax reform.
  2. The *assignats*.

E. Ecclesiastical legislation.
  1. Secularization of Church property.
  2. "Civil Constitution of the Clergy."
  3. Resulting Catholic opposition to the Revolution.

F. The Constitution of 1791.
  1. The separation of powers.
  2. Restriction of the suffrage.
  3. Position of the king in the new government.

G. Summary of the work of the National Assembly.
      Hayes, I, 479-486.

IV. The Limited Monarchy in Operation: The Legislative Assembly, 1791-1792.

A. Sources of opposition to the limited monarchy.
  1. The reactionaries.
    The emigrés.

The court: the flight to Varennes.

Conservative and Catholic peasants.

2. The radicals.

Conflict of interest between bourgeoisie and proletariat:
middle class and moderate nature of the reforms of
the National Assembly.

Center of radicalism in Paris.

The Clubs.

Propaganda.

Radical leaders: Marat, Danton, Robespierre.

3. Foreign enemies of the Revolution.

Nature and causes of foreign hostility to the Revolution.

The Holy Roman Emperor the champion of the old
régime.

Declaration of Pillnitz, August, 1791.

Attitude of the French toward the possibility of foreign
intervention.

B. Political parties in the Legislative Assembly.
  1. Members who voted independently.
  2. Feuillants.
  3. Jacobins: Girondists and the Mountain.

C. Outbreak of foreign war.
  1. Declaration of war against Austria and Prussia, April,
     1792.
  2. Early French reverses.
  3. Position of the royal family.
        Hayes, I, 486-500.

V. The First French Republic: The National Convention, 1792-1795.

A. Foreign invasion of France and the end of the limited monarchy.
  1. Proclamation of the Duke of Brunswick, July, 1792.
  2. The French reply: the insurrection of August 9-10, 1792.
  3. Suspension of the King and the call for a National Convention.
  4. An interval of anarchy.
  5. Tide of foreign invasion stemmed: Valmy.
  6. Proclamation of the Republic, September, 1792.

B. The National Convention and its achievements.
  1. Personnel of the Convention.

The Girondists.
The Mountainists.
The Plain.
2. Trial and execution of Louis XVI, January, 1793.
3. Prosecution of the foreign war.
    France the champion of revolution abroad as well as at
        home.
    The First Coalition (1793) : France on the defensive.
    Heroic endeavors of the revolutionaries.
        The nation in arms: military and administrative genius
            of Carnot.
        "Deputies on mission"; the new generals.
    French successes and the break-up of the First Coalition,
        1795.
4. Suppression of domestic insurrection.
    The Committee of Public Safety and "The Terror,"
        1793-1794.
    Thermidorian Reaction, 1794.
5. Social reforms.
    Radical character of the reforms of the Convention
        compared with moderate and middle-class reforms of
        the Constituent Assembly.
6. Eventual bourgeois control of the Convention.
7. Drafting of the constitution.
C. Constitution of the Year III: establishment of the "Directory."
    Hayes, I, 500-512.
    Map Study Number Seven (Part B).

VI. **Transformation of the Republic into a Military Dictator-
    ship: The Directory, 1795-1799.**

A. Weaknesses of the Directory.
B. The rising fortunes of Napoleon Bonaparte.
    1. His earlier part in the Revolution.
    2. The First Italian Campaign (1796-1797); **Treaty of**
        Campo Formio (1797).
    3. The Egyptian Campaign (1798).
C. Decline of the Directory.
    1. Financial and social disorders.
    2. The Second Coalition and French reverses in Europe.
    3. Bonaparte, the "Man of the Hour."

D. The end of the Directory.
    1. The *coup d'état* of the 18 Brumaire (1799).
    2. Promulgation of a new constitution: the Consulate.
        Hayes, I, 512-517.

VII. Significance of the French Revolution (1789-1799).

A. Conflicting interpretations of the revolutionary motto: "Liberty, Equality, Fraternity."
B. Permanent influence of the Revolution on European thought and society.
        Hayes, I, 517-519.

PART III: THE ERA OF NAPOLEON

I. The French Republic under the Consulate, 1799-1804.

A. The character and early career of Napoleon Bonaparte.
B. The government of the consulate: Constitution of the Year VIII.
    1. The Consuls, the Senate, the Tribunate, the Legislative Body.
    2. Napoleon as First Consul.
    3. The *plébiscite.*
C. Foreign war and the achievement of an advantageous peace.
    1. The second Italian campaign: treaty of Lunéville (1801).
    2. Dissolution of the Second Coalition.
    3. Treaty of Amiens, 1802.
D. Reforms under the Consulate: Napoleon "the son of the Revolution."
    1. Administrative centralization.
    2. Financial readjustment.
        Taxation and expenditures.
        The Bank of France (1800).
    3. Ecclesiastical settlement: the Concordat of 1801.
    4. Judicial reforms: the Code Napoléon.
    5. The new educational system.
    6. Public works and improvements.
E. Colonial ventures.
    1. Reacquisition of Louisiana (1800).

2. French campaign in Haiti.
3. Sale of Louisiana to the United States (1803).

F. Transformation of the Consulate into the Empire.
  1. Success of the Consulate and dwindling opposition to Napoleon.
  2. The plebiscite of 1802.
  3. The plebiscite of 1804.
    Hayes, I, 523-533.

II. The French Empire and Its Territorial Expansion.

A. Lapse of republican institutions.
  1. The court and the nobility.
  2. Monarchical alterations in dependent states.
  3. Censorship of the press and activity of the secret police.
  4. Eventual absolutism of Napoleon.

B. Renewal of foreign war and the expansion of the Empire.
  1. Formation of the Third Coalition: influence of Great Britain.
  2. Trafalgar (1805): continuation of British sea power.
  3. Defeat of Austria: Ulm and Austerlitz; Treaty of Pressburg (1805).
  4. Jena (1806): humiliation of Prussia.
  5. Defeat of Russia: Friedland; Treaty of Tilsit (1807).
  6. Humiliation of Sweden (1808-1809).
  7. Napoleon and his dynasty at the height of power.

C. Napoleon's achievements in the Germanies.
  1. Diminution in the number of states.
  2. Extinction of the Holy Roman Empire (1806).
  3. The Confederation of the Rhine.
  4. Extension to the Germanies of Revolutionary reforms.
    Hayes, I, 534-544, 577; Atlas: **Muir,** 11; **Robertson,** 8, 12, 14, 16, 20.
    Map Study Number Seven (Parts C and D).

III. Destruction of the French Empire.

A. Internal weaknesses of the Empire.

B. The economic war between France and Great Britain: "The Continental System."

1. The Berlin and Milan Decrees and the British Orders in Council.
2. Infringement on the rights of neutral nations.
3. Subordination of Napoleon's foreign policies to enforcement of the Continental System.

C. Nationalist resistance to the Napoleonic Empire.
1. Napoleon's interference in Portugal and Spain: the Peninsular War (1808-1813).
2. Premature efforts of Austria: Wagram (1809); terms of the peace.
3. The regeneration of Prussia.
   Influence of the French Revolution: social and economic reforms under Stein and Hardenberg.
   Military reform under Scharnhorst and Gneisenau.
   Educational reforms: von Humboldt.
   The spirit of nationalism: influence of Fichte and Arndt.
4. Renewal of war between France and Russia.
   Napoleon's Russian campaign and the retreat from Moscow.
   Results of the Russian campaign.
5. Final coalition against Napoleon: The War of Liberation.
   Leipzig, "The Battle of the Nations," October, 1813.
   Collapse of Napoleon's power outside of France.
   Campaign of 1814 in France; abdication of Napoleon.

D. The end of the Empire.
1. Restoration of the Bourbons in France: accession of Louis XVIII.
2. Monarchical restorations elsewhere in Europe.
3. Napoleon at Elba, 1814-1815.
4. "The Hundred Days" and the final overthrow of Napoleon: Waterloo (1815).
5. Napoleon at St. Helena, 1815-1821: beginnings of the "Napoleonic Legend."

> **Hayes, I,** 544-573; **Bassett,** 306-317; Atlas: **Muir,** 11, 19, 20b.

IV. Significance of the Era of Napoleon.

A. The Revolution perpetuated by the Empire.
1. "Liberty" under Napoleon.
2. "Equality" under Napoleon: permanent social achievements of the Empire.

3. "Fraternity" under Napoleon: impetus to nationalism and militarism in Europe.

B. Political readjustments in Europe.

C. Remarkable effects on Great Britain.
   Hayes, I, 573-577.

I. Continuation of the Conflict between Revolution and Reaction.

A. General nature of the conflict: revolutionary doctrines versus reactionary doctrines in the determination of social and political policies.

B. Alignment of social classes in the conflict.
   1. The reactionaries and conservatives.
   2. The revolutionaries and liberals.

C. Effect of the religious revival and the desire for peace.

D. The dominating personality of the era: Prince Metternich.
   Hayes, II, 1-5.

II. The Congress of Vienna, 1814-1815.

A. Royalty and aristocracy in control of the Congress.

B. Fundamental principles and their application in the settlement.
   1. "Legitimacy" and its applications.
   2. "Compensations" to the victors.

C. Reconstruction of the Germanies: the Germanic Confederation.

D. Instances of wilful disregard for the principle of nationality.

E. Critical estimate of the work of the Congress.
   Hayes, II, 5-10; Atlas: **Muir,** 12, 18b, 23d, 24b.
   Map Study Number Eight.

III. Alliances for the Preservation of Peace and Order.

A. General European acceptance of Metternich's policies.
   1. The maintenance of the *status quo.*
   2. The suppression of liberalism and revolution.

B. The Quadruple Alliance.
C. The Holy Alliance.
D. The Concert of the Great Powers.
    1. The protocol of Troppau (1820).
    2. International conferences, 1815-1822.
    3. The policy of intervention and its applications.
        Hayes, II, 10-14.

IV. Restorations and Reaction.

A. The Bourbon restoration in France.
    1. Louis XVIII and compromise with revolutionary ideas:
        the royal charter of 1814.
    2. Ultra-royalist reaction: the "White Terror."
    3. Control of the Moderate Royalists, 1816-1820.
    4. Return to power of the Ultra-Royalists, 1820.
    5. Continuance of royalist reaction under Charles X (1824-
        1830).
        Hayes, II, 14-20; Atlas: **Robertson, 9.**
B. The Bourbon restoration in Spain.
    1. The constitution of 1812.
    2. Ferdinand VII (1814-1833) and reaction.
    3. Revolt and temporary reversion to constitutionalism.
        Liberal opposition to the King: insurrection of 1820.
        Congress of Verona (1822) and European intervention.
        Restoration of absolutism.
    4. Revolution in the Spanish colonies.
        British policy: Canning and non-intervention.
        American policy: the Monroe Doctrine.
        Break-up of the Quadruple Alliance.
        Hayes, II, 20-26, 47.
C. Reaction in Portugal.
    1. Anti-British revolution of 1820 and return of the royal
        family.
    2. Defection and independence of Brazil (1822).
    3. Factional strife and the triumph of absolutism.
        Hayes, II, 26-28.
D. Tory reaction in Great Britain.
    1. Tory control of the British government.
        Contrast between liberal policy abroad and conservatism
        at home; explanation of this seeming inconsistency.

Effect of the French Revolution: repression of liberalism and shelving of reform.

The Napoleonic Wars and Tory prestige.

Tory leaders: George IV (1820-1830); Castlereagh; Wellington.

2. Class legislation under the Tories: inclosures; Corn Laws.
3. Sources of opposition to the Tory reaction.

"Intellectual Radicals."

Roman Catholics and Protestant Dissenters.

The industrial classes.

4. Economic distress and popular discontent.
5. The "Manchester Massacre" and the Six Acts (1819).
6. Undermining of reaction: policies of Canning, Huskisson, Peel.

Hayes, II, 28-37.

E. Trial and abandonment of liberal administration in Russia.
   1. Liberal experiments of Alexander I (1801-1825).
   2. Metternich and the conversion of Alexander to reaction.
   3. The Decembrist revolt and the accession of Nicholas I (1825).
   4. Continued reaction under Nicholas I (1825-1855).

Hayes, II, 37-41.

F. Maintenance of autocracy in Central Europe.
   1. Metternich and reaction in the Austrian dominions.
   2. Metternich and reaction in the Germanic Confederation.

      Opposition to constitutionalism.

      Persistence of liberal agitation: *Tugendbund* and *Burschenschaft.*

      Repressive measures: the Carlsbad Decrees, 1819.

   3. Metternich and reaction in the Italian states.

      Liberalism in the Italian states: the *Carbonari.*

      Suppression of the uprising in Naples, 1820.

      Unsuccessful uprising in Piedmont, 1821.

      Hayes, II, 41-46; Atlas: **Muir,** 18b, 23d.

V. Failure of Metternich's Policies and Partial Triumph of Liberalism.

A. Foreign policy of Great Britain and the disintegration of the Quadruple Alliance.

B. The Greek insurrection (1821-1832).

1. Premature uprising of 1821 : leadership of Ypsilanti.
2. The War of Greek Independence (1821-1829).
   European sympathy for the Greeks.
   Foreign intervention and the Battle of Navarino (1827).
   Russo-Turkish War (1828-1829).
   Foundation of the Greek Kingdom.

C. Revolutionary movements of 1830.
   1. The July Revolution in France.
      Middle class opposition to the government of Charles X.
      The July ordinances and the outbreak of revolt.
      Overthrow of Charles X and accession of Louis Philippe, "King of the French."
      Effects of the July Revolution in Europe.
   2. The Belgian Revolution.
   3. Unsuccessful revolts in the Germanies and in the Italian states.
   4. Suppression of the Polish revolt of 1831.

D. The end of the era of Metternich.

Hayes, II, 46-57, 130-131; Atlas: Robertson, 10, 13, 17.

Book IV

DEMOCRACY AND NATIONALISM

PART I. THE INDUSTRIAL REVOLUTION

I. Introduction.

A. Far-reaching results of the Industrial Revolution as compared with the French Revolution.

B. Basic elements of the Industrial Revolution.
   1. The invention and application of machinery to the processes of mining, manufacturing, agriculture, and transportation.
   2. Utilization of artificial power,—water, steam, electrical, etc.
   3. Fundamental changes in the organization of industry.
       Sub-division of labor, standardization, and large scale production.
       The factory system and the extension of capitalistic organization.

C. Circumstances favoring the Industrial Revolution in England, 1770-1825.
       Hayes, II, 67-69.

II. The Mechanical Inventions.

A. The inventions in the textile industries.
   1. Kay's fly shuttle (1738).
   2. Hargreaves and the spinning jenny (1770).
   3. Arkwright and the water frame (1769).
   4. Crompton's mule (1779).
   5. Cartwright's power loom (1785).
   6. Whitney's cotton gin (1792).

B. Development of the steam engine and applications of steam power.
  1. Pioneers in development of the steam engine.
  2. James Watt (1736-1819).
    Improvements in Watt's engine.
    Construction of steam engines for the market.
  3. General adaptation of the steam engine.
C. Continuity of the Industrial Revolution.

> Hayes, II, 69-75; Gibbins, *Industry in England,* 341-357.

III. Economic Effects of the Industrial Revolution.

A. General economic effect: tremendous expansion of economic activity.
  1. Development of industry.
  2. Increase in commerce.
  3. Phenomenal increase in wealth.
  4. Accumulation of "surplus wealth,"—capital.
B. General social effect: growth and redistribution of population.
C. The factory system and capitalism.
  1. Effect of the mechanical inventions on the disintegration of the "domestic system" of manufacture.
  2. Realignment of social classes.
    Economic importance and social position of industrial capitalists.
    Altered position of the urban workers: the proletariat.
  3. Acute social problems resulting from the factory system.
D. Political and social reactions to the new conditions.
  1. Attitude of the government.
    Vain attempts to enforce outworn mercantilist regulations.
    Era of non-interference: *laissez-faire*.
  2. Attitude of social philosophers: the "new economics."
    Tenets of "economic individualism."
    Program of "economic individualism."
      Freedom from governmental restrictions.
      Freedom of competition.
      Freedom of contract.
    Results of "economic individualism."
    The emancipation of industry.

"Liberty": results to capitalists and to wage-earners.
Unrelieved misery of the workers.
3. Opposition to "economic individualism."
Utopian socialists: Owen, Saint-Simon, Fourier.
Government ownership socialists: Louis Blanc.
Christian socialists: Maurice, Kingsley.
   Hayes, II, 75-88; **Gibbins,** *Industry in England,*
   381-426.
   Map Study Number Nine and Supplements (*ad lib.*).

IV. Immediate Effects of the Industrial Revolution upon Politics.

A. The new rôle of the bourgeoisie.
1. Increased wealth and prestige of the middle class.
   The older bourgeoisie.
   The new industrial capitalists.
2. Political ambitions of the bourgeoisie.
3. Economic motives for these political ambitions.
4. Rising political influence of the bourgeoisie.

B. Middle class political achievements in England.
1. The Reform Bill of 1832.
2. The Municipal Corporations Act, 1835.
3. Repeal of the Corn Laws, 1846.
   Middle class opposition to the Corn Laws.
   The Anti-Corn Law League.
   Breach in the Conservative Party and repeal of the Corn Laws.

C. The middle class monarchy of Louis Philippe in France.
1. Rôle of the bourgeoisie in the Revolution of 1830.
2. Dependence of the monarchy upon middle-class support.
3. Middle class political achievements under Louis Philippe (1830-1848).

D. Middle class achievements in the Germanies.
1. Backwardness of the industrial revolution in the Germanies.
2. Achievement of economic union: the Zollverein (1833).

E. Political and social readjustments in the United States.
1. The American industrial revolution.
2. Railway construction and the opening of the West.
3. Class and sectional divisions on the protective tariff.

4. Beginnings of the American labor movement.
>   Hayes, II, 88-97; Bassett, 341-350, 463-465, 680-
>   683, 741-744; Atlas: Muir, 43, 44, 57.

PART II. DEMOCRATIC REFORM AND REVOLUTION, 1830-1848

I. Democracy and the Industrial Revolution.

A. Democracy and the growth of the democratic spirit.
1. Debt to Christianity.
2. Debt to the French Revolution.
3. Debt to the Industrial Revolution.

B. New conditions make democracy a practical program.
>   Hayes, II, 100-102.

II. Political and Social Reforms in Great Britain.

A. Removal of religious disabilities.
1. Repeal of the Test and Corporation Acts (1828).
2. Daniel O'Connell and Catholic Emancipation (1829).

B. Parliamentary reform.
1. The champions of reform.
2. Coercion of the Lords and the passage of the Reform Bill
    of 1832.
3. Provisions of the Reform Bill of 1832.
4. New political parties in the reformed parliament.
5. Popular dissatisfaction with the Reform of 1832: the
    Chartist movement.
    The "Six Points" of Chartism.
    Chartist demonstration of April, 1848.
    Failure of Chartism.
    Persistence of Chartist principles.

C. Social legislation.
1. Tory reforms, 1820-1829.
    Influence of Peel, Huskisson, and Canning.
    Revision of the criminal law; legalization of trade unions
    (1824); removal of religious disabilities.
2. Provisions and underlying principles of the Poor Law of
    1834.
3. Public grants for education.

4. Prison reform.
5. Abolition of slavery in the colonies.
6. Industrial legislation.
   Influence of Lord Ashley.
   The Factory Act of 1833.
   The Mines Act of 1842.
   Hayes, II, 101-116; **Cross,** 633-643.

III.   The Democratic Revolution of 1848 in France.

A. Growing opposition to the monarchy of Louis Philippe.
    1. Sources of opposition to the July monarchy.
        Legitimists, Republicans, Catholics, Socialists.
        Division of the middle class: Thiers versus Guizot.
        Questions of foreign policy.
        Question of reform of the franchise.
    2. Increasing demand for electoral reform: the "banquets."

B. The February Revolution (1848).

C. The Second French Republic (1848-1852).
    1. First phase: problems of the working class.
        The "national workshops."
    2. Second phase: the republic of the middle classes.
        Election of the Constituent Assembly.
        Abolition of the national workshops.
        The "June Days."
        Work of the Constituent Assembly: the Constitution of
        the Republic.
        Hayes, II, 116-123.

IV.   The Revolutionary Movements of 1848 in Central Europe.

A. Interacting forces of nationalism and liberalism.

B. First phase of the revolutionary movements: the liberal and
    nationalist revolutions.
    1. Contagion of the February revolution in Paris: the down-
        fall of Metternich.
    2. Spread of the revolutionary movement, 1848.
        March revolutions in Italy.
        March revolutions in the Germanies.
        Meeting of the *Vorparlament* at Frankfort.
        Revolution in Austria, March-May, 1848.

March revolution in Hungary.

3. Nationalism a disrupting force in the revolutionary movements.

Nationalism in the Austrian Reichstag.

The Pan-Slav Congress.

Serbo-Croats versus Hungarians: Jellachich.

Nationalist rivalries in the Frankfort Assembly.

C. Second phase of the revolutionary movements: the republican revolts, October, 1848, to June, 1849.

    1. Failure of the proletarian insurrection in Vienna, October, 1848.

    2. Proclamation of the Hungarian Republic, April, 1849.

    3. Republican outbreaks in Italy and the Germanies.

D. The triumph of reaction.

    1. Failure of the republican revolts.

Restoration in Italy.

End of the Hungarian Republic, July, 1849.

Renunciation of constitutionalism and reform in Austria.

Suppression of republicanism in the Germanies.

    2. Failure of the Frankfort Assembly to achieve German unification.

    3. Restoration of the Germanic Confederation (1851).

    4. Conservative character of the Prussian constitution of 1850.

E. Significance of the revolutionary movements of 1848-1849.

Hayes, II, 123-144; Atlas: **Muir,** 12, 18b, 23d, 25a; **Robertson,** 13, 17, 18, 21.

PART III. THE GROWTH OF NATIONALISM, 1848-1871

I. Louis Napoleon Bonaparte and the Erection of the Second French Empire.

A. Early career of Louis Napoleon Bonaparte.

    1. His relationship to the great Napoleon.

    2. His education and formulation of his political ideas.

    3. Premature attempts to seize the French government.

    4. The Revolution of 1848 as his great opportunity.

B. Prince Louis Napoleon as President of the Second French Republic (1848-1852).

1. Louis Napoleon, politician.
2. Conflict between President and Assembly.
3. The *coup d'état* of December, 1851.

C. Erection of the Second French Empire.
  1. The constitution of January, 1852.
  2. Proclamation of the Empire, December 2, 1852: Napoleon III.
  3. Conciliation of class interests.
  4. New French imperialism.
  5. Underlying strength of the Empire: economic prosperity; nationalism.
  6. Fundamental weakness of the Empire: militarism.
     The Crimean War (1854-1856) : the cost to France.
     Hayes, II, 149-163; Atlas: **Robertson,** 9.

II. The Political Unification of Italy.

A. Nationalism in the Italian states.
  1. Programs for the unification of Italy.
     Mazzini and the Republicans.
     The Clericals and Conservatives, advocates of federalism.
     The Liberal Monarchists, favoring a monarchy under King of Sardinia.
  2. Weakness of the Republicans and the Clericals.
  3. Strength of the Liberal Monarchists.
     Prestige of Sardinia.
     Liberalism of Sardinia: constitution of 1848.
     Sardinian patriots: Victor Emmanuel, Garibaldi, Cavour.

B. Cavour's policies the foundation of Italian unity.
  1. Liberal reform in Sardinia, 1850-1859.
  2. Foreign policy as an aid to Italian unification.
     Sardinian participation in the Crimean War.
     Interview with Napoleon III at Plombières: the alliance with France.

C. French intervention in Italy: the war of 1859.
  1. Successes of the French and Sardinians: Magenta and Solferino.
  2. Outbreak of popular revolutions in northern Italy; Louis Napoleon's change of heart.
  3. The armistice of Villafranca (1859).
  4. The plebiscites in Tuscany, Parma, Modena, and Romagna.

    5. The Treaty of Turin (1860).
       Gains of Sardinia.
       Cession to France of Nice and Savoy.
D. The completion of Italian unification.
    1. Garibaldi and the annexation of the Two Sicilies (1860).
    2. Annexation of Umbria and the Marches (1860).
    3. Proclamation of the Kingdom of Italy (1861).
    4. Acquisition of Venetia (1866).
       The alliance with Prussia.
       The Seven Weeks' War.
       The plebiscite.
    5. Occupation of Rome (1870).
    6. Rome the capital of Italy (1871).
           Hayes, II, 163-175; Atlas: Muir, 18b; Robertson,
           17.
           Map Study Number Ten.

III.   The Decline of the Second French Empire.

A. Beginnings of opposition to Louis Napoleon in France.
    1. French intervention in Italy and its reaction on domestic
       politics.
    2. Concessions to liberalism, 1860.
    3. The Polish Insurrection of 1863: French reception of
       Napoleon's policy of non-intervention.
B. The Mexican expedition (1862-1867).
    1. Glory abroad designed to still dissatisfaction at home.
    2. Maximilian, Emperor of Mexico, 1864-1867.
    3. Collapse of the Mexican adventure.
    4. The Mexican affair a boomerang against Napoleon.
C. Growing opposition to Louis Napoleon.
    1. Sources of opposition.
    2. Further concessions to liberalism, 1869.
D. Final attempt to preserve the Empire: the war with Germany
   (1870).
           Hayes, II, 175-180.

IV.   The Political Unification of Germany.

A. The problem of German unification.
    1. Obstacles in the way of German unification.
       The Germanic Confederation.

Austrian participation in German affairs.
Particularism of the princes.
Failure of liberalism as a unifying force.
2. Prussia as a leader.
Prestige of Prussia.
Leadership in Prussia: William I (1861-1886) ; Otto von
   Bismarck (1815-1898).
3. Prussian preparation for leadership in German affairs.
The constitutional conflict in Prussia, 1861-1863.
   The proposed army reforms of Moltke and Roon.
   Parliamentary opposition : the Progressive Party.
   Bismarck as "tamer" of the Prussian parliament.
Achievement of thorough-going military reform.

B. The extrusion of Austria and the dissolution of the Germanic
   Confederation.
   1. The Schleswig-Holstein question and the war of 1864
      with Denmark.
   2. The dispute between Austria and Prussia over disposition
      of the duchies.
      The Convention of Gastein (1865).
      Diplomatic isolation of Austria by Bismarck.
   3. The Seven Weeks' War (1866).
      Defeat of Austria: Sadowa.
      The Treaty of Prague and the dissolution of the Con-
      federation.
   4. Effects of the Seven Weeks' War upon Austria.
      Final destruction of the system of Metternich.
      Exclusion of Austria from participation in German and
         Italian affairs.
      Concessions to liberalism in Austria: the constitution of
         1861 superseded by the *Ausgleich* (1867), establish-
         ing the Dual Monarchy of Austria-Hungary.
      Austrian imperialist interests diverted to the Balkans.

C. Formation of the North German Confederation (1867), forerunner of the German Empire.
   1. Prussian annexations, 1866, and their significance.
   2. Constitution of the North German Confederation.
   3. Independent position of the south German states.
   4. Bismarck's concessions to liberalism.
      The National Liberal Party in Germany and its rela-
      tions with Bismarck.

D. The Franco-German War and the final achievement of German unification.
  1. Demands of Louis Napoleon III for "compensations" and the diplomatic isolation of France by Bismarck.
  2. The underlying cause for war: French nationalism versus German nationalism.
  3. The pretext for war: the Hohenzollern candidature for the Spanish throne.
  4. The Franco-German War (1870-1871).
     Metz and Sedan.
     Downfall of Napoleon III and proclamation of the Third French Republic.
     Surrender of Paris, January, 1871.
     Treaty of Frankfort, 1871.
  5. Proclamation of the German Empire, at Versailles, January, 1871.
  6. Effects of the Franco-German War upon Europe.
     The Treaty of Frankfort a prelude to the Great War of 1914.
     End of the temporal rule of the Pope with the occupation of Rome by Victor Emmanuel.
     Denunciation by Russia of the neutralization of the Black Sea.
       Hayes, II, 180-204; Atlas: **Muir,** 23d, 24b, 52b; **Robertson,** 13, 14.
       Map Study Number Eleven.

V. National Unification in the United States.

A. Growth of sectionalism.
  1. Economic and social divergence of North and South.
  2. Differences of opinion as to the constitutional powers of Congress.

B. Sources of sectional friction.
  1. The tariff controversy.
  2. The slavery controversy.

C. The Civil War (1861-1865).
  1. The election of 1860 and the secession of the Southern states.
  2. The Confederacy: constitution and territorial extent.

3. Broadening of the issues of the war: the Emancipation Proclamation.
4. Military superiority of the North and the triumph of the unionists.

D. Political and economic reconstruction of the South.
Bassett, 350-352, 384-388, 511-518, 577-581, 619-638.

VI. Summary of the Growth of Nationalism, 1848-1871.

A. Astounding achievements of nationalism in central Europe.

B. Growth of democracy concomitant with the growth of nationalism.

C. Continued growth of nationalism after 1871.
Hayes, II, 204-206.

PART IV. SOCIAL FACTORS IN RECENT EUROPEAN HISTORY

I. "The Era of the Benevolent Bourgeoisie."

A. Chief characteristics of the era, 1871-1914.
  1. Beginning of new governments in many European countries.
     The German Empire.
     The Third French Republic.
     The Dual Monarchy of Austria-Hungary.
     The British government after the Reform Bill of 1867.
     Other governments.
  2. Definitive triumph of the principles of the French Revolution.
     Nationalism.
     Constitutionalism.
     Middle class "liberty" and "equality."
  3. Preëminence of the middle class.

B. Bourgeois character of the era.
  1. Influence on social and economic institutions of the Industrial Revolution.
  2. Altered relations of other classes to the bourgeoisie.
  3. Bourgeois devotion to the principles of the French Revolution.

C. General statement of the practical achievements of the era, 1871-1914.

D. Dissenters from the spirit of the era: Clericals and Socialists. **Hayes, II,** 211-223.

II. Christianity and Politics.

A. General character of the religious controversies of the era 1871-1914.
   1. Divisions of religious opinion.
      Extremists: Clericals and anti-clericals.
      Position of the great mass of the people.
   2. Reasons for acute character of the conflict in Roman Catholic countries.
      Catholic dogma compared with Protestant.
      Catholic organization compared with Protestant.

B. Political opposition to the Catholic Church.
   1. Catholic attitude toward the principles of the French Revolution.
   2. Reactionary character of the pontificate of Pius IX.
      Papal attack on the established social order.
      The encyclical *Quanta Cura* and the *Syllabus of Errors* (1864).
   3. The Vatican Council (1869-1870) and the dogma of papal infallibility.
   4. Rapid growth of anti-clericalism.

C. Intellectual opposition to the Catholic Church. (See below, *Christianity and Science.*)
      Hayes, II, 223-230.

III. The New Science.

A. General characteristics of science in the nineteenth century.
   1. Far-reaching development of experimental science.
   2. Extensive utility of applied science.
   3. Development of the theory of evolution and philosophical science.

B. Science and scientists of the nineteenth century.
   1. The *Cosmos* of Alexander von Humboldt.
   2. The new geology: work of Sir Charles Lyell.

Principles of Geology (1830-1833) : the uniformitarian
theory.
Geological Evidences of the Antiquity of Man (1863).
3. The theory of evolution.
Influence of Malthus and Lyell.
Charles Darwin: *On the Origin of Species* (1859) and
subsequent work.
Alfred Wallace and his rôle in the formulation of the
Darwinian theory.

C. Popularization and application of the new science.
1. The *Synthetic Philosophy* of Herbert Spencer.
2. Thomas Huxley's attacks on revealed religion.
3. Ernest Renan and "higher criticism."
Hayes, II, 230-240.

IV. Christianity and Science.

A. Protestantism and the new science.
1. The new science an attack on the fundamentals of Protestant theology.
2. Effect of science upon the Protestant churches and
theology.
Protestant compromise between science and religion.
Exceptions to the Protestant compromise.
3. Divisions in the Anglican church as typical of the reaction of Protestantism to science.
The Oxford Movement and the "high church" party.
The "low church" party.
The "broad church" party.

B. The Catholic Church and the new science.
1. Seemingly irreconcilable conflict between Catholic Christianity and the new science.
2. The pontificate of Leo XIII and a "working compromise"
with science.
Revived study of mediæval theology and the formulation
of a Catholic view of Darwinism.
Encouragement of research in church history.
Papal patronage of natural science.
The work of Louis Pasteur and Gregor Mendel.
3. Leo XIII and the new social order.
Political principles of Leo XIII.

Social program of Leo XIII: the encyclical *Rerum Novarum* (1891).
4. "Modernist" tendencies in the Catholic Church.
C. Relative position of Clericals and Anti-Clericals in the twentieth century.
  Hayes, II, 240-252.

V. The Social Problem and the Decline of Laisser-faire.

A. Bourgeois liberalism and the decline of *laisser-faire*.
  1. Middle class acceptance of limited governmental regulation of industry.
  2. The tendency toward "social legislation."
B. Karl Marx and the rise of modern Socialism.
  1. Early socialism.
    Babeuf.
    Utopian socialism: Fourier, Saint-Simon, Owen.
    Government ownership socialism: Louis Blanc.
  2. Karl Marx and the development of "scientific" socialism.
    Early life and training of Karl Marx.
    Association with Friederich Engels: the *Communist Manifesto* (1848).
    Karl Marx in England and the elaboration of his socialist theories: *Das Kapital*.
    Significance of Karl Marx and his work.
  3. The tenets of Marxian socialism.
  4. The practical program of Marxian socialism.
  5. Organization of the new Socialism.
    "The International."
    National Socialist parties.
    Ferdinand Lassalle and the Social Democratic Party in Germany.
    Other national parties.
  6. Sources of opposition to Socialism.
  7. Division among the Socialists on questions of political tactics.
C. Anarchism and Syndicalism.
  1. The forerunner of modern Anarchism: William Godwin.
  2. Philosophical Anarchism: the work of Pierre Joseph Proudhon.
    Life of Proudhon.

Nature and tenets of Proudhonian Anarchism.
The weakness of philosophical Anarchism: extreme individualism.
3. Revolutionary Anarchism: the work of Mikhail Bakunin.
The Russian revolutionary, Bakunin.
The terror as a weapon against capitalistic society.
Break between Anarchism and Socialism.
4. Syndicalism, a modern form of revolutionary Anarchism.
Hayes, II, 252-271.

PART V. THE UNITED KINGDOM OF GREAT BRITAIN AND IRELAND, 1867-1914

I. The Breakdown of the Victorian Compromise.

A. The nature of the Victorian Compromise, 1832-1867.
  1. Concessions of the aristocracy to middle class liberals.
  2. Concessions of middle class liberals to the aristocracy.
  3. Common program of conservatives and liberals: opposition to further extension of political democracy; continued disfranchisement of the workers.

B. Reasons for the breakdown of the Victorian Compromise.
  1. The legacy of Chartism: growing strength of the democratic spirit and the demand for political and social reform.
  2. Trade unionism and labor agitation.
  3. Rivalry of political parties for popular support.
    Hayes, II, 277-278.

II. Political Reform in the United Kingdom.

A. The political situation leading to the Reform of 1867: parties and party leaders.
  1. William Ewart Gladstone and the political principles of the Liberal Party.
  2. Benjamin Disraeli and the adoption of a constructive program by the Conservatives.
  3. John Bright and reform agitation among the industrial classes.
    Political principles of Bright.
    Influence of the American Civil War on reform agitation.

60 AN OUTLINE OF MODERN HISTORY

Alliance between Bright and Gladstone.
4. Failure of the Liberal Reform Bill of 1866.

B. The Reform of 1867.
  1. Disraeli and the Conservative Reform Bill: reasons for the "leap in the dark."
  2. Provisions of the Act of 1867.
    Redistribution of representation.
    Readjustment of qualifications for the suffrage.
  3. Extent to which the Act was a democratic measure.

C. Extension of reform under Gladstone and the Liberals.
  1. Representation of the People Act, 1884.
  2. Redistribution of Seats Act, 1885.
  3. Partial achievement of the "Six Points of the Chartists."

D. Curbing of the power of the aristocracy.
  1. Undemocratic character of the House of Lords.
  2. The Parliament Act of 1911 as a step toward political democracy.
    Hayes, II, 278-290; **Cross,** 752-760.

III. The Government of the United Kingdom.

A. The British government as the product of a series of historical compromises.
  1. Evolutionary character of the British Constitution.
  2. Survivals of undemocratic authority.
    The Crown, a relic of absolutism.
    The House of Lords, a relic of feudalism.
    Nominal and actual powers of Crown and Lords.
  3. Popular representation.
    Evolution of the House of Commons in the direction of democracy.
    Increasing power of the Commons.
  4. Beginnings of the cabinet system.

B. The parliamentary system of government.
  1. Relations between crown, cabinet, and parliament: the principle of "ministerial responsibility."
  2. Efficiency of the cabinet system.

C. Centralized regulation of local government.
    Hayes, II, 290-297.

IV. British Political Parties.

A. Political reform and the transformation of political parties.
  1. Effect of the Reform Bill of 1832 on Whigs and Tories.
  2. Effect of the Victorian Compromise on party issues.
  3. Effect on Liberals and Conservatives of the breakdown of the Compromise.

B. The Unionist Party.
  1. Coalition of Liberal Unionists and Conservatives (1895).
  2. Membership and principles of the Unionists: leadership of Joseph Chamberlain.
  3. Revival of the tariff controversy: the demand for "imperial preference."

C. The Labor Party.
  1. Reasons for the formation of the Labor Party.
  2. Organizations supporting the Labor Representation Committee, 1900.
  3. Growth of the Labor Party.

D. The Liberal Party.
  1. Circumstances favoring the regeneration of the Liberal Party after the death of Gladstone.
      Agrarian discontent: influence of Henry George.
      Revival of the tariff controversy.
      The Boer War.
  2. Ideals of the new Liberalism.
  3. The coalition with the Labor and Irish Nationalist Parties.
  4. Achievements of the new Liberalism, 1906-1914.

E. The Irish Nationalist Party.
      Hayes, II, 297-307.

V. British Social Legislation.

A. Measures designed to maintain the standard of living.
  1. Factory and mines acts.
  2. Minimum wage for workers in sweated industries: the Trade Boards Act, 1909.
  3. Minimum wage for miners: the Minimum Wage Act of 1912.
      Theory of the act: justice or a minimum of decency?
      Altruism and efficiency as motives.

    4. Adoption of the principle of workmen's compensation, 1897-1906.
    5. Measures for the welfare of children.
    6. Old age pensions instituted, 1908.
    7. Attack on unemployment.
       The Labor Exchange Act, 1909.
       The National Insurance Act, 1911.
    8. General Welfare provisions of the National Insurance Act.

B. Measures designed to develop and maintain the independence of the worker.
    1. Promotion of education.
    2. Encouragement of trade unionism and legalization of wider trade union activities.

C. Measures designed to reduce inequalities in the distribution of wealth.
    1. The Lloyd George budgets: extent of taxation on incomes, inheritances, unearned increment, luxuries.
    2. Land reform.
       Housing and Town Planning Act (1909).
       Small Holdings and Allotments Act (1907).
       Taxation of landlords.
    3. Unrealized Liberal program of land reform, 1913-1914.
       Hayes, II, 307-319.

VI. The Irish Question.

A. Dissatisfaction in Ireland with British rule.
    1. Ecclesiastical grievances of the Irish Catholics.
    2. Agrarian discontent: absentee landlordism.
    3. Irish nationalism.

B. The British government and reform in Ireland.
    1. Ecclesiastical.
       Disestablishment of the Church of Ireland (1869).
    2. Agrarian.
       The Tenant-Right League and the "Three F's."
       Land Act of 1870.
       Second Irish Land Act (1881).
       Land Purchase Act of 1891.
       Local Government Act (1898).

3. Political: movement for home rule for Ireland.
   Gladstone's Home Rule Bills of 1886 and 1893.
   The Home Rule Bill of 1912.
   Rôle of the Irish Nationalist Party and John Redmond.
   Attitude of Ulsterites and Unionists: Sir Edward
   Carson.
   Passage of the Home Rule Act, 1914.
   Outbreak of the Great War and the suspension of Irish
   home rule.
   Hayes, II, 319-326; Atlas: **Muir,** 42.

PART VI. LATIN EUROPE, 1870-1914

I. The Third French Republic.

A. The making of the Republic.
   1. Revolutionary proclamation of September 4, 1870; the
      Provisional Government.
   2. Government of the National Assembly, 1871-1875.
      Parties in the Assembly: position of the Monarchists.
      Peace with Germany: the Treaty of Frankfort and its
      provisions.
      Rebellion of the Commune of Paris: its causes and
      significance.
      The Rivet Law (1871): the Assembly and Thiers.
      Financial and military reforms.
      Administrative reform: organization of local govern-
      ment.
      Question of the form of government.
      Divisions among the Monarchists: Imperialists, Legiti-
      mists, Orleanists.
      The Chambord Incident (1873).
      Acceptance of the Republic: the Constitutional Laws
      of 1875.
   3. The conflict for control of the Republic and the triumph
      of Republicanism.
      Factions in the government of the Republic.
      Marshal MacMahon and the Monarchists.
      Gambetta and the Republicans.
      Gambetta and the political principles of "Moderate"
      Republicanism.

Republican control of the Senate (1879).

Final triumph of Republicanism: the presidency of Jules Grévy.

B. The government of the Republic.
   1. Delegation of powers under the constitution.
       The French parliament: the Champer of Deputies and the Senate.
       The President: nominal powers.
       The Ministry and the supremacy of the parliament.
   2. Comparison between the French constitution and the American and British constitutions.
   3. The local government of France.

C. Bourgeois character of the Republic.
   1. Middle-class interests of French statesmanship.
   2. Promotion of economic prosperity.
   3. French imperialism under the Republic.
       Colonial expansion and development.
       Motives: economic, religious, nationalist.
   4. Social legislation.
       Motives.
       Important measures.
   5. Guarantees of individual liberties.

D. Repression of Clerical and military opposition to the Republic.
   1. Education policy of the Republic: the Ferry Laws.
   2. The Boulanger episode and its reaction on militarism, Monarchism, and Clericalism.
   3. The Dreyfus Affair.
       Anti-Semitism and the case of Captain Dreyfus.
       Vindication of Dreyfus and its effect upon militarism and Clericalism.
   4. The Associations Act (1901).
   5. Separation of Church and State (1905).
   6. The Compromise of 1907.

E. The political groups in France.
   1. The "group system" in France and the question of "instability" of ministries.
   2. Political parties and alignments, 1900-1910.
       The "Right": Monarchists; the Action Libérale.
       The "Left": the Unified Socialists.
       The "Center": the Bloc.

Progressists.
Radicals.
Radical Socialists.
Anti-Clericalism as a political issue.
3. Political issues in 1913.
4. The elections of 1914 and a realignment of political groups.
The Unified Radicals.
The Federation of the Left.
Hayes, II, 331-367; Atlas: **Robertson, 6, 9.**

II. The Kingdom of Italy.

A. Problems of social and economic unification.
  1. Contrasts between the North and the South.
  2. Industrial backwardness and the economic policy of the government.
  3. The burden of taxation.
  4. Illiteracy: the education law of 1877.
  5. Emigration.
B. The government of the Kingdom.
  1. Italy a centralized state.
  2. Constitutional and parliamentary government.
  3. The electoral laws of 1882 and 1912.
C. Problems of the relation of Church and State.
  1. Special and peculiar nature of the ecclesiastical problem in Italy.
  2. The Law of Papal Guarantees (1871) and the *non expedit.*
  3. Recent relations between Church and State.
D. Political parties and the government of Italy, 1870-1914.
  1. The Régime of the Right, 1870-1876.
  2. The Régime of the Left, 1876-1896.
  3. Liberalism in Italy, 1896-1914.
  4. Parties of opposition: Clericals, Republicans, Socialists, Syndicalists.
E. Foreign policy: nationalism and irredentism.
Hayes, II, 367-378; Atlas: **Robertson, 6, 17.**

III. Spain.

A. Events leading to the establishment of constitutional government in Spain.

1. The Carlist War and the reign of Isabella II.
2. The Revolution of 1868 and the period of anarchy, 1868-1875.
3. Restoration of the Bourbons: Alphonso XII (1875-1885).
4. The Constitution of 1876.

B. Spain under Alphonso XIII (1886-   ).
1. The regency of Maria Christina (1885-1902).
   The Cuban revolt (1895-1898).
   The War with the United States (1898) and its results.
2. Personal rule of Alphonso (1902-   ).
   Economic development of Spain.
   Liberal legislation as an antidote to political opposition.
   Imperialism: Spain in Morocco.
   Hayes, II, 378-385.

IV. Portugal.

A. Decline of the monarchy in Portugal.
1. Politics under the monarchy, 1852-1889.
2. The disastrous reign of Carlos I (1889-1908) and the dictatorship of Franco.
3. Manoel II (1908-1910) and the downfall of the monarchy.

B. Portugal under the republic.
1. The republican revolution of 1910.
2. Instability of the Republic and political repression.

C. The Portuguese colonial empire.
   Hayes, II, 385-389.

V. The Kingdom of Belgium.

A. The Belgian constitution of 1831.

B. Economic prosperity of Belgium: development of agriculture, industry, commerce.

C. Supremacy of the Catholic Party in Belgium, 1884-1914.
1. Relations between Church and State.
2. Opposition to the Catholic Party.
   The issue: public education.
   Parties of opposition: Liberals; Socialists.
3. Belgian educational policy.
4. Extension of political democracy.
5. Social legislation.

D. World politics: Belgium's part in the Great War.
  1. Beginnings of the Belgian colonial empire: Leopold II and the Congo.
  2. The military service law of 1909 and the armament bill of 1913.
  3. King Albert (1909-   ) and Belgian resistance to the German invasion.
     Hayes, II, 389-392.

PART VII. TEUTONIC EUROPE, 1871-1914

I. The German Empire.

A. The constitution and government of Germany, 1871-1918.
  1. The government of the German Empire.
     The Emperor.
       Powers as Emperor.
       Powers as king of Prussia.
     The Bundesrat.
     The Reichstag.
  2. Relations between the federal government and the state governments.
  3. Undemocratic character of the German government.
     Privileged position of Prussia in the Empire.
     Powers of the Imperial Chancellor.
     Powers of the Bundesrat.
  4. Reasons for the stability of the German government.

B. The Empire under Bismarck, 1871-1890.
  1. Consolidation of the Empire, 1871-1877.
  2. Political parties under Bismarck.
     National Liberals.
     Conservatives.
     Progressives.
     Catholics (Center).
     Social Democrats.
  3. Bismarck's conflict with the Catholics: the *Kulturkampf*.
  4. Bismarck's war on Socialism, 1878-1890.
  5. Bismarck's new economic policy: the abandonment of *laisser-faire*.
     Break with the National Liberals.

The protective tariff of 1879.

Beginnings of the German colonial empire, 1884-1885.

Social legislation, 1881-1890.

6. Accession of William II (1888-1918). Dismissal of Bismarck (1890).

C. The Empire under William II, 1890-1914.
  1. Economic prosperity: growth of industry, commerce, population.
  2. Growth of parties of opposition.
      Growth of the Social Democratic Party; reasons for this growth.
      Minor political groups of opposition: Guelfs, Danes, Alsace-Lorrainers, Poles.
      The case of the Poles: Prussian treatment of Polish subjects.
  3. Chancellorship of Caprivi (1890-1894) and agrarian dissatisfaction.
  4. Prince Hohenlohe as chancellor (1894-1900) : Germany a "World Power."
      Renewed activity in the acquisition of colonies.
      Imperial encouragement and protection of German investments abroad.
      Beginnings of the powerful German navy.
  5. Chancellorship of Bülow (1900-1909).
      The tariff of 1902.
      The *Bloc.*
      Foreign policy under Bülow.
      The decisive elections of 1907.
  6. Bethmann-Hollweg, Chancellor 1909-1917, and the Great War.
      The Army Bill of 1913.
      Seeming solidarity of the German people in 1914.
      Hayes, II, 397-426; Atlas: **Robertson,** 13.

II. The Dual Monarchy of Austria-Hungary, 1867-1914.

A. The constitution and government of Austria-Hungary.
  1. The Emperor-King Francis Joseph (1848-1916).
  2. The joint government of Austria and Hungary: the *Ausgleich.*
  3. The government of Austria: the *Reichsrat.*

4. The government of Hungary: the Magnates and the
   Deputies.
   Position of Transylvania and Croatia-Slavonia.
5. Relations between Austria and Hungary.
   Conflicts over domestic policies.
   Agreement on foreign policy: the Balkans and the
   question of Bosnia-Herzegovina.

B. Political and social reforms in Austria.
   1. Extension of political democracy: the electoral laws of
      1896 and 1907.
   2. Formation and development of political parties.
   3. Social legislation.
   4. The problem of conflicting nationalities.

C. Reactionary policies of the Hungarian government.
   1. Economic and political repression of Rumans and Serbo-
      Croats.
   2. Undemocratic character of the suffrage.
   3. Increasing demand for political and social reform.
      Hayes, II, 426-435; Atlas: **Robertson, 18, 21.**

III. The Swiss Confederation.

A. Diversity of languages and religions.
B. The government of Switzerland.
   1. The Constitution of 1848.
   2. The Constitution of 1874 and the extension of federal
      power.
   3. Radical extension of political democracy in the cantons
      and in the confederation: the initiative and referen-
      dum; other political experiments.

C. Economic and social progress.

D. National defence: the "Swiss system" of universal training in
   the militia.
      Hayes, II, 435-439; Atlas: **Robertson, 15.**

IV. The Kingdom of the Netherlands.

A. The Dutch kingdom and its colonial empire.
B. Holland under King William III (1849-1890).

C. Holland under Queen Wilhelmina (1890-   ).
    1. Holland and the problem of military preparedness.
    2. Economic prosperity of the Dutch people.

D. The neighboring grand-duchy of Luxemburg.
        Hayes, II, 439-442.

V. The Scandinavian States.

A. Developments common to the Scandinavian nations.

B. The Kingdom of Denmark.
    1. The constitution of 1866 and the government of Denmark.
    2. Frederick VIII (1906-1912), Christian X (1912-   ), and
        the extension of political democracy in Denmark.

C. Personal union of Sweden and Norway (1815-1905).
    1. The Bernadotte dynasty.
    2. Differences between Sweden and Norway.
    3. Achievement of the independence of Norway, 1905.

D. The kingdom of Norway and the kingdom of Sweden since
    1905.
    1. Extension of political democracy.
    2. Social and economic problems.
        Hayes, II, 442-446; Atlas: Robertson, 31.

PART VIII. THE RUSSIAN EMPIRE, 1855-1914

I. Russia under Alexander II (1855-1881).

A. Heritage from Nicholas I.
    1. Unyielding opposition of Nicholas to liberalism.
    2. Russia a land of the old régime.
    3. Military defeat: the Crimean War (1854-1856).
    4. The demand for reform.

B. Reforms of Alexander II, 1855-1865.
    1. Emancipation of the serfs.
        Serfdom in Russia: miserable condition of the peasantry.
        Reform of the agrarian system: the Decree of 1861.
        Abolition of serfdom.
        Distribution of land to the *mirs.*
        Faulty administration of the decree.

    2. Local self-government.

        The *Zemstvos:* composition and powers under the Decree of 1864.

    3. Legal and judicial reforms: the Decree of 1862.

C. Abandonment of liberalism and the return to reactionary policies, 1865-1881.

    1. Immediate cause of reaction: the Polish revolt of 1863.

    2. Institution of the secret police and the repression of liberalism.

    3. Adoption of compulsory universal military service (1874).

D. The rise of revolutionary parties.

    1. Nihilists.

    2. Anarchistic Socialists.

    3. Terrorists.

E. Assassination of Alexander II (1881).

        Hayes, II, 452-460; Atlas: **Muir,** 27, 63; **Robertson,** 28-30, 36.

II. Autocracy and "Russification," 1881-1905.

A. Devotion of Alexander III (1881-1894) and Nicholas II (1894-1917) to autocracy, nationalism, and Orthodoxy.

B. Factors contributing to the maintenance of the autocracy in Russia.

    1. Heterogeneity of peoples composing the Russian Empire.

    2. Intrenchment of the autocracy in Russia.

        Philosophy and practice of reaction: Pobêdonostsev and Plehve.

        Loyalty of the governing classes.

        Support of the Orthodox Church.

        Illiteracy and the lack of popular education.

        Filial devotion of the peasantry to the Tsar.

        Predominance of agriculture and the maintenance of conservatism.

        Repressive measures of the government.

        The tradition of the autocracy.

    3. Intimate association of the autocracy with Pan-Slavism.

C. Pan-Slavism and "Russification" under Alexander III.

    1. Two-fold program of Pan-Slavism.

        "Russification" of the Empire.

Extension of Russian influence to foreign lands inhab-
ited by peoples of Slavic race.
2. Suppression of lesser languages and dissident religious
faiths.
In Poland, White Russia, Lithuania, and the Baltic
Provinces.
Persecution of the Jews: repressive legislation and
pogroms.

D. Continuance of autocracy and "Russification" under Nicholas II.
Hayes, II, 460-473; Atlas: **Muir,** 26b.

III. The Industrial Revolution in Russia and Revival of Opposition to the Autocracy.

A. The Russian industrial revolution.
1. Phases of the industrial revolution: commerce, industry,
railways.
2. Reasons for the occurrence of the revolution in the last
part of the nineteenth century.
3. Comparative industrial backwardness of Russia and the
continued predominance of agriculture.

B. New problems created by the industrial revolution; their partial
solution.
1. Problem of government's relationship to the new industrial classes.
2. Liberal policies of Witte, 1892-1903.
Encouragement of railway construction.
The protective tariff.
Capitalistic imperialism: Russian influence in China and
Persia.
3. Opposition of the autocracy to further economic liberalism.

C. New forms of opposition to the maintenance of the autocracy.
1. Demand of the landed classes for agricultural and political
reforms.
2. Rise of a class-conscious proletariat.
Influence of Marxian Socialism and the organization of
Socialist parties: Social Democrats and Socialist
Revolutionaries.
3. The middle classes and the development of a new
liberalism.
The "Liberators."

4. Reaction against "Russification": opposition and resistance of the lesser nationalities.
   Hayes, II, 473-478.

IV. The Revolutionary Movement of 1905 and the Duma, 1906-1914.

A. Causes of the revolutionary movement.
   1. Effect of the Russo-Japanese War (1904-1905).
   2. "Red Sunday" and its results.

B. Concessions of Nicholas II to the revolutionaries.
   1. The October Manifesto (1905) and the establishment of
      the Duma.
   2. Dismissal of reactionary ministers and the recall of Witte.

C. The decline of the revolutionary movement, 1906, and the
   triumph of reaction.
   1. Factions among the revolutionaries.
      Milyukóv and the "Cadets."
      The "Octobrists."
   2. "Union of the Russian People": the "Black Hundreds"
      and the reactionary terror.
   3. The manifesto of March, 1906; limitation of the powers
      of the Duma.
   4. Dismissal of Witte. The premiership of Stolypin (1906-
      1911).

D. Struggle of the Duma to establish parliamentary government.
   1. Dissolution of the First Duma: the Viborg Protest (1906).
   2. Dissolution of the Second Duma; alteration of the elec-
      toral law by decree of the Tsar, 1907.
   3. Conservative character of the Third Duma (1907-1912):
      moderate reforms.
   4. Election of the Fourth Duma, 1912.

E. The revolutionary movement in Finland.
   1. The "national strike" of 1905.
   2. The Finnish constitution of 1906.

F. Russia on the eve of the Great War.
   1. Pan-Slavism and militarism: the Balkan crises and the
      army bill of 1913.
      Hayes, II, 478-487.

PART IX. THE DISMEMBERMENT OF THE OTTOMAN EMPIRE

I. Decline of the Ottoman Empire, 1683-1815.

A. High tide of the Turkish advance: the Ottoman Empire in 1683.

B. Decline of the Ottoman Empire in the seventeenth and eighteenth centuries.
   1. Gains of Austria: the Treaty of Karlowitz (1699).
   2. Gains of Russia: the Treaty of Kuchuk Kainarji (1774).
   3. Corruption and tyranny in the administration of the Christian provinces of the Sultan.
   4. Extent of the Ottoman Empire in 1815.

C. Rise of nationalism in the Balkan Peninsula.
   1. Balkan races and nationalities.
   2. Nationalist propaganda.
      Literary.
      Ecclesiastical: the religious situation in the Balkans.
      Political.

> Hayes, II, 490-498; Atlas: **Muir**, 28, Fig. XXII; **Robertson**, 5, 18, 22, 23.

II. The Great Powers and the Dismemberment of Turkey in Europe, 1815-1886.

A. First fruits of nationalism in the Balkans.
   1. Independence of Montenegro (1799).
   2. Autonomy of Serbia (1830).
   3. Independence of Greece (1832).
   4. Autonomy of the Rumanian provinces (1829).
   5. Union of Moldavia and Wallachia as Rumania (1862).

B. The advance of Russia in the Near East.
   1. Russian aims and policies in the Near East.
   2. The Crimean War (1854-1856) a temporary check to the Russian advance.
   3. The Russo-Turkish War of 1877-1878.
      Occasion: disorders in European Turkey, 1875-1876.
      Military defeat of the Turks.
      The Treaty of San Stefano, 1878.
   4. Intervention of the powers and the demand for a general congress to consider the Eastern question.

C. The Congress of Berlin and the revision of the Treaty of San
Stefano: the Treaty of Berlin, 1878.
1. Interests of Austria and Great Britain and the attitude of
Bismarck.
2. The Treaty of Berlin, 1878.
Gains of Russia.
Status of Bosnia-Herzegovina.
British occupation of Cyprus.
Autonomy of Bulgaria, not including Eastern Rumelia
and Macedonia.
Independence of Rumania, Serbia, and Montenegro.
Cession of Thessaly to Greece.
Paper reforms for Turkey.

D. Temporary character of the Berlin settlement.
Hayes, II, 498-509; Atlas: Robertson, 23, 24.

III. The Autonomy of Crete and Loss of the Turkish
Possessions in Africa.

A. Loss of Crete.
1. Repeated Cretan revolts against the Turks.
2. The Græco-Turkish War, 1897, and the autonomy of
Crete.
3. Union of Crete with Greece, 1913.

B. Loss of the African possessions.
1. Egypt.
Mehemet Ali, "Hereditary Governor," 1841.
Egypt under a *khedive*, 1866-1914.
The independent sultanate of Egypt, 1914.
2. French conquest of Algeria (1830-1847) and Tunis (1881).
3. The Turco-Italian War and the loss of Tripoli (1912).
Hayes, II, 509-514; Atlas: Robertson, 5, 26, 35.

IV. Progress of the Balkan Nations and the Attempt
to Rejuvenate Turkey.

A. Progress of the Balkan nations in the latter half of the nineteenth century.
1. Greece.
Constitutional government under George I (1863-1913).
Economic prosperity and nationalist aspirations.

Statesmanship and diplomacy of Venizelos (1864-   ).
Constantine I (1913-1917 and 1920-   ).
2. Rumania.
King Charles (1866-1914).
Nationalist aspirations.
Natural resources and economic prosperity.
3. Serbia.
The court revolution of 1903 and the accession of King
Peter.
Nationalist aspirations of the Serbs.
4. Montenegro.
5. Bulgaria.
Economic development.
Nationalist aspirations of the Bulgars.
Russian interference in Bulgarian affairs.
Ferdinand, "Tsar of the Bulgars," 1908.

B. Abdul Hamid II (1876-1909) and opposition to reform in
Turkey.
1. Temporary concessions to the demand for reform.
The Constitution of 1876.
Paper guarantees of the Treaty of Berlin, 1878.
2. Reaction and the abrogation of the Constitution of 1876.
3. The régime of Abdul Hamid.
Problem of the public debt.
Loss of Turkish territory.
Disorders and civil war.
Foreign influence and intervention.

C. Attempted reorganization of the Turkish Empire.
1. The "Young Turks" and the movement for reform.
2. The revolution of 1908: establishment of constitutional
government.
3. The revolution of 1909: deposition of Abdul Hamid.
4. Policies of the Young Turks.
Conflicts between liberalism and the new nationalism.
5. Foreign difficulties of the revolutionary government.
Loss of Bosnia-Herzegovina and of suzerainty over
Bulgaria (1908).
The Turco-Italian War (1911-1912) and the Balkan
Wars (1912-1913).
Hayes, II, 515-528.

V. The Balkan Wars.

A. The First Balkan War.
1. The Macedonian and Albanian questions and the Balkan alliance.
2. Military operations and the defeat of the Turks.
3. The Treaty of London (1913).

B. The Second Balkan War.
1. Cause: quarrels among the Allies over the Turkish spoils.
2. Military operations: intervention of Rumania and Turkey.
3. The Treaty of Bucharest and the Treaty of Constantinople (1913).

C. Results of the Balkan Wars.
1. Territorial readjustments in the Balkans.
2. Costs of the wars.
3. Decline of European Turkey.
4. Intensification of nationalism in the Balkan States.

D. Rival interests of the Great Powers in the Near East.

E. The Balkan Wars the forerunner of the Great War of 1914.
Hayes, II, 528-539; Atlas: Robertson, 25, 26.
Map Study Number Twelve (Part A).

Book V

NATIONAL IMPERIALISM

3. The capitalist system and the new imperialism.
  Influence of capitalists in the promotion of the new imperialism.
  Surplus capital and the "backward regions" as opportunities for profitable investments. The so-called "export of capital."

B. The French Revolution, the growth of nationalism, and the new imperialism: the patriotic motive.
  1. Colonies for national power and prestige.
  2. Colonies as homes for surplus population.
    Questionable validity of the "surplus population" argument.

C. The religious motive.
  1. Spread of Catholic and Protestant missions.
  2. Effects of missions on imperialism; effects of imperialism on missions.

D. Reaction of the new imperialism on nationalism and on democracy.
  Hayes, II, 550-560.

PART II. THE SPREAD OF EUROPEAN CIVILIZATION IN ASIA

I. The Partial Dismemberment and the Political Regeneration of the Chinese Empire.

A. Isolation of the Chinese Empire before 1840.

B. Territorial extent of the Chinese Empire at the opening of the nineteenth century.

C. Forcible opening up of China to foreign commerce and Christian missions.
  1. The Opium War (1840-1842) and the Treaty of Nanking.
  2. The Second Chinese War (1856-1860) and the treaties of Tientsin.
  3. Extension of "open-port" privileges to other powers.

D. Foreign aggression and the loss of the outlying provinces and tributary states.
  1. Russia: Sakhalin, Amur River region, Sin-Kiang.
  2. Japanese aggrandizement.
    Japanese recognition of Korean independence (1876).

The Chino-Japanese War of 1894-1895.

Treaty of Shimonoseki (1895).

Revision of the Treaty of Shimonoseki by the Powers.

3. European gains, 1897-1898: the leased ports and other concessions.

Germany in the Shan-tung peninsula: Kiao-chau.

France in Kwang-chow Wan.

Russia in Manchuria and the Liao-tung peninsula: Port Arthur.

Great Britain in Wei-hai-wei.

4. The Russo-Japanese War (1904-1905) and the Treaty of Portsmouth.

5. Other foreign territorial encroachments.

The French in Indo-China.

The British in Burma and Tibet.

E. Opening up of China to foreign capitalists.

1. Railway and factory construction; exploitation of natural resources.

2. Foreign "spheres of influence."

F. Political regeneration of China.

1. China's problem: Europeanization or partition?

2. Early attempts at reform and Europeanization.

3. Reaction and the Boxer rebellion (1900).

4. The Young China Party and the Revolution of 1911-1912.

5. Establishment of the Chinese Republic, 1912.

Hayes, 11, 560-576; **Atlas: Muir,** 63; **Robertson,** 34.

II. The Awakening of Japan.

A. The ending of Japanese seclusion: visits of Perry (1853) and Harris (1857).

B. The Japanese revolution of 1867-1868.

1. Factors contributing to the outbreak of the revolution.

Shogun versus Mikado and the conversion of the Daimios.

Question of the necessity of Europeanization.

Shintoism.

2. Overthrow of the Shogun and accession as Mikado of Mutsuhito (1867-1912).

3. Abolition of feudalism.

4. The revolution the forerunner of reform.
   Military.
   Administrative.
   Political: adoption of constitutional government (1889).
   Adoption of occidental methods and ideas.

C. The industrial revolution in Japan.
   1. Remarkable developments in commerce, industry, and railway construction.
   2. Social effects of the industrial revolution.

D. Militarism and imperialism.
   1. The War with China (1894-1895) and the annexation of Formosa.
   2. Preparedness: military reforms and naval construction.
   3. The Russo-Japanese War (1904-1905).
      Military and naval events: Mukden and Port Arthur.
      Treaty of Portsmouth and the annexation of part of Sakhalin.
   4. Annexation of Korea (1910).
   5. The Anglo-Japanese Alliance (1902).
   6. Japan a World Power.
      Hayes, II, 577-586; Atlas: **Muir,** 52c, 63; **Robertson, 34.**

III. Russian Expansion in Asia.

A. Extension of the frontier and boundaries of Siberia.

B. Russian expansion southward.
   1. From Siberia: encroachments on Chinese Manchuria and Mongolia.
   2. In the Caspian region and Turkestan.
   3. In Persia.

C. The clash with Great Britain in central Asia.
   1. Conflicting interests in Persia.
      The struggle for commercial and political concessions.
      The Persian Revolution of 1906-1909 and foreign intrigue.
      The agreement of 1907 defining "spheres of interest."
   2. The agreement of 1907 regarding Afghanistan.
      Hayes, II, 586-592; Atlas: **Muir,** 63; **Robertson,** 32-34.

IV. Survey of the Rival Empires in the Far East, 1914.

A. European.
  1. Russian: extent, resources, and weaknesses of the Russian possessions.
  2. British possessions and influence.
  3. French, Dutch, and German colonial empires.
B. American.
  1. Colonial possessions of the United States in the Far East.
  2. American policies in Asia.
     Commercial: the "open door" in China.
     Financial: official discouragement of investments and concessions during early years of the Wilson administration.
C. Asiatic.
  1. Japanese territorial expansion at the expense of China.
  2. Japan as the champion of Asiatic peoples against the "foreigner." A Japanese Monroe Doctrine for Asia?
     Hayes, II, 592-596; Atlas: **Muir, 63; Robertson, 34.**

PART III. EUROPEAN CIVILIZATION IN THE AMERICAS

I. The Old Colonialism and the New Imperialism.

A. Achievements of the old colonialism in America.
  1. The transmission of French and English civilization to Canada.
  2. Anglo-Saxon civilization in the United States.
  3. Latin civilization in Central and South America.
B. Beginnings of the new imperialism.
     Hayes, II, 600-602.

II. The Development of the United States.

A. Territorial expansion and the growth of population.
B. The industrial revolution in the United States.
  1. Influence of the War of 1812 and its antecedents.
  2. Industrial progress and railway construction before the Civil War.

    3. The Civil War a new industrial revolution.
    4. Effects of the industrial revolution.
        On domestic problems.
        On foreign policy: naval construction and imperialism.

C. The United States a World Power.
    1. Effect of the War with Spain: a foothold for the new
        imperialism in the Far East and in the West Indies.
    2. The Monroe Doctrine and the special position of American
        investors in Latin America.
    3. Construction of the Panama Canal.
            Hayes, II, 602-605; **Bassett,** 764-774, 782-790, 806-
            807, 809-821, 826; Atlas: **Muir,** 57.

III. Latin America and Its Problems.

A. Political problems of Latin America.
    1. Tardiness in the achievement of political independence
        (1810-1903).
    2. The ten Latin-American states of 1830 and the twenty of
        1914.
    3. The remnants of European holdings in Latin America.
    4. Governmental instability: the problem of "revolution" and
        war.
    5. Possibilities for the solution of these problems: example
        of the "A-B-C" powers.
    6. Problem of relationship with the United States: the Mon-
        roe Doctrine and Pan-Americanism.

B. Economic problems of Latin America.
    1. The plantation system and the persistence of a landed
        aristocracy.
    2. Lack of capital and necessity for foreign investments.

C. Mexico as an example of the political and economic problems of
    Latin America.
            Hayes, II, 605-614; Atlas: **Muir,** 58.

PART IV. THE PARTITION OF AFRICA

I. Preliminary Steps in the Partition of Africa.

A. Limited European settlements before 1870.
    1. Early Portuguese and Dutch settlements.
    2. Beginnings of the British dominion.
        Encroachments on the Dutch possessions: annexation of Cape Colony (1806) and of Natal (1843).
        British possessions in West Africa.
    3. French ventures.

B. Important results of the abolition of the African slave trade (1807-1850).

C. Exploration and European interest in the interior of the Dark Continent.
    1. Stanley and Livingstone.
    2. Leopold II and the Congo Free State: foundation of the Belgian colonial empire.
        Hayes, II, 614-620.

II. Staking Out of Claims by the Powers.

A. Motives in the partition of Africa.
    1. Rôle of the missionaries and patriots.
    2. Rôle of the promoters and concessionaires: Rhodes and Lüderitz.
    3. Rôle of the governments.

B. The partition of Africa by international agreements.
    1. The international conference of Berlin (1884-1885).
    2. The Anglo-German agreement of 1890.
    3. Disputes between France and Great Britain and their settlement.
        The Anglo-French agreement of 1890.
        The Fashoda incident (1898) and the Anglo-French agreement of 1899.
        The Anglo-French agreement of 1904.
    4. Disputes between France and Germany: the Moroccan question.
        The Algeciras Conference (1906).

The Agadir affair (1911).

The French agreements of 1911 and 1912 with Germany and Spain.

5. The Anglo-Portuguese agreement of 1891.

C. Survey of the possessions and colonial policies of the European powers in 1914.

Hayes, II, 620-637; Atlas: **Muir,** 64; **Robertson,** 35.

PART V. THE BRITISH EMPIRE

I. Self-Governing Colonies.

A. The nature and relative importance of the self-governing colonies.

B. Canada.
1. The government of Canada, 1774-1837.
2. The French Canadians of Lower Canada and the Rebellion of 1837.
3. Lord Durham's report, 1839.
4. Achievement of responsible government (1847). A precedent for the extension of self-government to other colonies.
5. Establishment of the Dominion of Canada (1867). Constitutional provisions of the British North America Act.
6. Territorial expansion of Canada.

C. Australia.
1. The Australasian colonies and the Australian Commonwealth Act, 1900.
2. Social and labor legislation in Australia.

D. New Zealand.
1. Establishment of the Dominion of New Zealand (1907).
2. Experiments in political and social democracy.
3. State socialism in New Zealand.

E. South Africa.
1. Responsible government in Cape Colony (1872) and Natal (1893).
2. The Boer War (1899-1902): British annexation of the Orange Free State and the Transvaal.

3. Extension of self-government to the former Boer republics (1906-1907).
4. The Union of South Africa established, 1909.

F. The movement for imperial federation.
1. The relationship between the Dominions and the mother country: slight British control over the "colonial nations."
2. Imperial preference an economic bond of union: the work of Chamberlain.
3. Imperial conferences a political bond of union.
4. Dominion contributions to naval and military defence of the Empire.

> Hayes, II, 640-657; Atlas: **Muir,** 57, 64d, 65; **Robertson,** 36.

II. Crown Colonies and Protectorates.

A. Fundamental differences between the crown colonies and protectorates and the self-governing colonies.
B. The British crown colonies.
C. Territories administered by chartered companies.
D. The protectorates.
1. The nature of a protectorate.
2. British protectorates in Asia and Africa.
3. The special position of Egypt.
Events leading to the establishment of the protectorate (1914).
The Suez Canal and the strategic importance of Egypt.
British reforms in Egypt and the extension of partial self-government.
The Young Egyptian movement.
Administration of the Anglo-Egyptian Sudan.
E. Undemocratic administration of the crown colonies and protectorates.

> Hayes, II, 657-662.

III. The Empire of India.

A. The position of India in the British Empire.
B. Disunity in India.
1. Geographical divisions a hindrance to homogeneity.

2. Racial divisions.
3. Religious differences.
4. Political dissensions.
5. Relation of Indian disunity to the maintenance of British rule.

C. Extension of British control and the evolution of the government of India.
   1. The empire-builders of the East India Company.
   2. Indian government under the East India Company.
      Gradual extension of control by the British Parliament: the Regulating Act of 1773 and the India Act of 1784.
      The Sepoy Mutiny (1857) and the end of Company government.
   3. Indian government under the Crown.
      Better Government of India Act, 1858.
      The Queen "Empress of India," 1877.
      Indian Councils Act, 1909.
   4. Spread of Nationalist agitation.

D. Economic importance to Great Britain of the control of India.

E. Economic progress of India under British rule.
        Hayes, II, 662-672; Atlas: **Muir,** 62, 63; **Robertson,** 36.

IV. The British Empire Illustrative of the New Imperialism.

A. Imperialism and British business.
   1. British manufacturers and imperialism.
   2. The British commercial classes and the colonies.
   3. British capitalists and the profits of colonial investments.

B. The "parasites of imperialism."

C. Imperialism and militarism.
   1. The British Navy and the British Empire.
   2. The military classes and the imperial impulse.

D. The success of Great Britain in empire-building.
        Hayes, II, 672-675.

PART VI. INTERNATIONAL RELATIONS, 1871-1914

I. The Concert of Europe.

A. Failure of the organization of a Concert of Europe (1830), but persistence of the principle.

B. Achievements of the Concert of Europe.
1. The Declaration of Paris (1856) and the development of the laws of war.
2. The Geneva Convention and the International Red Cross.
3. The Congress of Berlin (1878) and the Near Eastern question.
4. Attempts of the Concert to adjust colonial controversies.
5. The Concert and the Boxer Rebellion (1900).
6. Weakness of the Concert during the Balkan Wars (1912-1913).

C. Forces operating in support of the principle of the Concert.
1. Growing popular internationalism and pacifism.
2. Extension of the principle of international arbitration.
3. The Hague Peace Conferences (1899 and 1907).

D. Forces operating in opposition to the principle of the Concert.
1. Nationalism.
2. Grave territorial problems.
3. Militarism.
4. The cult of nationalism and militarism.

E. Decline of the Concert of Europe.
1. Rise of the idea of a Balance of Power.
2. Importance of the armament bills of 1913.
3. Collapse of the Concert in the crisis of 1914.
          Hayes, II, 679-691.

II. The Hegemony of Germany, 1871-1890.

A. Bismarck and the isolation of France.
1. Alienating European sympathy and support of France.
    Conciliation of Austria-Hungary.
    Bismarck and Great Britain.
    Bismarck's policy toward Russia.
2. Alliances to secure the diplomatic isolation of France.
    The Three Emperors' League, 1872.

The Dual Alliance with Austria-Hungary, 1879.
Formation of the Triple Alliance, 1882.

B. The success of Bismarck's policies.
    Hayes, II, 691-697.

III. The Balance of Power, 1890-1914.

A. Reaction against the hegemony of Germany and the formation
    of the Triple Entente.
    1. Formation of the Dual Alliance between Russia and
        France, 1891-1895.
        Reasons for the break between Russia and Germany.
        Reasons for the alliance between Russia and France.
    2. British abandonment of the policy of isolation.
        Reasons for growing rivalry of Great Britain and Ger-
        many.
        Sources of conflict between Great Britain and the mem-
        bers of the Dual Alliance.
        The Anglo-Japanese Alliance, 1902.
    3. The Entente Cordiale of 1904 between England and
        France.
        Importance of the policies of Delcassé.
    4. Formation of the Triple Entente, 1907.
B. The Triple Entente and the diplomatic isolation of Germany and
    Austria-Hungary.
    1. Re-establishment of friendly relations between Russia
        and Japan and the renewal (1911) of the Anglo-
        Japanese alliance.
    2. French conciliation of Italy and Spain.
C. Trials of strength between Triple Alliance and Triple Entente.
    1. The Moroccan question.
        First Moroccan crisis: Tangier and Algeciras (1905-
        1906).
        Second Moroccan crisis: the affair of Casablanca (1908).
        Third Moroccan crisis: the Agadir incident (1911).
    2. The Near Eastern question.
        German and Austrian ambitions in the Near East: the
        Drang nach Osten and the Bagdad Railway.
        First Near Eastern crisis: annexation of Bosnia-
        Herzegovina (1908) and the humiliation of Russia
        and Serbia (1909).

Second Near Eastern crisis: the Tripolitan War (1911-1912).

Third Near Eastern crisis: the Balkan Wars (1912-1913).

D. The ordeal by fire.
1. 1913, the year of preparations.
2. The final test of strength: the Great War.
   Hayes, II, 697-719.
   Map Study Number Twelve (Parts B and C).

Book VI

THE GREAT WAR

I. The General Cause: International Anarchy.

A. Nationalism.
1. Nationalism as an obstacle to international organization.
2. Exclusiveness and intolerance of nationalism: *Kulturs*, racial egotism and antipathies, "perils."
3. Nationalism in uncritical support of foreign trade and foreign investments.

B. Imperialism.
1. Competition and self-interest the keynotes of the age.
2. Trade and investment international in fact, national in organization.
3. Spread of imperialism and the appearance of an increasing number of "arenas of friction."

C. Militarism.
1. Force and the threat of force the final arbiters in international differences: The Armed Peace.
2. Professional diplomacy the handmaid of militarism.
   Hayes, III, 1-7.

II. The Immediate Cause: Nationalism, Imperialism, Militarism in Germany.

A. Factors in the development of militarism in Germany.
1. Geographical situation.
2. The tradition of militarism.
3. Political organization of Prussia and of the German Empire.
4. Structure of German society.

93

B. German imperialism.
   1. Classes in support of imperialism: influence of the *Junkerthum* and capitalists.
   2. Half-hearted resistance of the Catholics and Social Democrats.

C. Relationship of German nationalism to imperialism and militarism.

D. Aggressive German foreign policy.
   1. The "mailed fist" in the Moroccan and Near Eastern crises.
   2. Aggressiveness and the doctrine of a "preventive war."
      Hayes, III, 7-13.

III. The Occasion: Murder of the Archduke Francis Ferdinand.

A. The Austro-Serbian crisis.
   1. Political significance of the murder of the Archduke Francis Ferdinand, at Serajevo, June 28, 1914.
      Domestic and foreign policies of the Archduke.
      Alleged connivance of the Serbian Government with the assassins.
   2. The Potsdam conference and the determination of Austro-German policy.
   3. The negotiations between Austria and Serbia.
      The Austrian ultimatum of July 23, 1914.
      Character of the Serbian reply, July 25.
      Austrian declaration of war, July 28.

B. Failure of diplomacy in the crisis.
   1. Attempts to adjust the Austro-Serbian controversy.
   2. Efforts to avoid a general European war.
      Proposals of England, France and Russia.
      Mediation and a conference of the Powers.
      Demands of Germany.
      Localization of the conflict between Austria and Serbia.
      Cessation of military preparations by other nations.
   3. Pressure of the militarists against the diplomatists: mobilization and the outbreak of war.

C. Casting of the die: the resort to force.
    1. Russian mobilization and the German declaration of war, August 1.
    2. The German ultimatum to France and the German declaration of war, August 3.
    3. Violation of the neutrality of Belgium and the intervention of Great Britain, August 4.
    4. Alignment of the combatants, August 13.
       Germany and Austria-Hungary.
       Russia, France, Great Britain, Serbia, Montenegro, Belgium.
    5. Proclamations of neutrality by Italy and the United States.
       Hayes, III, 13-20.

PART II. MILITARY AND DIPLOMATIC EVENTS OF THE WAR

I. Events of the Fall and Winter, 1914-1915.

A. Mobilization and the German plan of campaign.

B. The war on the Western front.
    1. The German thrust through Belgium.
       Fall of Liège and other fortresses: influence of the new artillery.
       Futile resistance of the French at Charleroi and of the British at Mons.
    2. Failure of the French counter-thrust in Alsace-Lorraine.
    3. The invasion of France.
       High tide of the German advance and the first Battle of the Marne, September 6-12.
    4. The German drive against Antwerp and the channel ports.
    5. Summary of German gains and losses in the West.
       Hayes, III, 21-40.
       Map Study Number Thirteen.

C. The war in the East.
    1. The Russian invasion of East Prussia.
       Tannenberg, August 26-31.
    2. The Russian invasion of Galicia.
    3. The German invasion of Russian Poland: the struggle for Warsaw.

4. Manifestations of the weaknesses of the Russian autocracy in prosecution of the war.
   Hayes, III, 41-53.

D. Successful Serbian resistance to Austrian invasion.
   Hayes, III, 55-57.

E. Conquest of the German colonies.
   1. Participation of Japan and seizure of the German rights in Shan-tung.
      Reasons for the Japanese declaration of war, August 23.
      Siege and capture of Kiao-chao, November 10.
   2. Importance of the loyalty of the British colonies.
   3. Seizure by Australia, New Zealand and Japan of Germany's island colonies in the South Seas.
   4. Attacks on the German possessions in Africa.
      Hayes, III, 62-69.

F. The war on the high seas.
   1. Importance of the British naval power.
   2. The German naval victory in the southern Pacific, November 1, 1914.
   3. Battle of the Falkland Islands, December 8.
   4. German raiders: against British commerce and against the English seacoast.
   5. Beginning of the German submarine warfare: announcement of the "war zone" and the blockade of France and the British Isles, February, 1915.
      Question of the legality of submarine warfare.
      Protests of the neutrals.
      Events leading to the sinking of the *Lusitania,* May 7, 1915, and effect upon public opinion in the United States.
      Hayes, III, 58-62, 73-79.

G. Readjustment of international alliances and widening of the conflict.
   1. The Pact of London (September, 1914).
   2. Enlistment of Turkey by the Central Powers.
      Economic and strategic importance of Turkey.
      Events leading to the Allied declarations of war, November 3-5, 1914.
      Proclamation of the Holy War: the test of strength between nationalism and Mohammedanism.

British annexation of Cyprus (November) and establishment of the protectorate over Egypt (December).
Weaknesses of Turkey as a belligerent.
Hayes, III, 20, 69-73.

II. Rising Fortunes of Germany, 1915-1916.

A. Efforts of the Allies in the Near East.
  1. The disastrous Dardanelles campaign, February, 1915, to
     January, 1916.
  2. Failure of the Allied diplomatic offensive in the Balkans.
  3. The intervention of Italy.
     Italian demands on Austria-Hungary for "compensa-
     tions."
     The secret treaty with the Entente, April 26, 1915.
     Declaration of war against Austria-Hungary, May 23,
     1915.
     Advantages and disadvantages to the Allies of Italian
     participation.
     Hayes, III, 80-98.

B. Anglo-French offensives in the West, 1915.
  1. The British at Neuve Chapelle, March, 1915.
  2. The lesson of Neuve Chapelle: Allied deficiencies in mu-
     nitions.
  3. The German counter-offensive: Second Battle of Ypres,
     April-May, 1915; first use of poison gas.
  4. Allied offensives of September in the Artois and in the
     Champagne.
  5. Influence of campaigns in the West on the Russian retreat.
     Hayes, III, 112-120.

C. The Austro-German offensive of 1915 against Russia.
  1. Mackensen's drive: the recovery of Galicia.
  2. Hindenburg's drive: the conquest of Russian Poland.
  3. Weaknesses of Russia.
     Deficiencies in *matériel*.
     Political and social discontent.
     Hayes, III, 99-107.

D. German mastery of the Near East.
  1. The German diplomatic offensive in the Balkans: Bul-
     garia's entry into the war, October, 1915.

2. Conquest of Serbia, October-November, 1915.
3. Belated attempt of the Allies to assist Serbia: the Salonica expedition.
4. *Mittel-Europa* and the *Drang nach Osten* accomplished facts.
5. Turkey in the war.
   Abortive British expedition in Mesopotamia: siege of Kut-el-Amara and surrender of Townshend.
   The Grand Duke Nicholas in the Caucasus.
6. Belligerency and defeat of Rumania, August-December, 1916.
   Hayes, III, 121-142; 181-191.

E. Teutonic efforts to force a decision in 1916.
   1. Teutonic optimism in the spring of 1916 and its causes.
   2. Great effort under the Prussian Crown Prince at Verdun, February-July.
      Strategic and political importance of Verdun.
      Heroic defence of the French; ultimate failure of the Germans.
   3. The Austrian offensive in the Trentino and its partial success.
   4. The offensive at sea.
      Declaration of "unrestricted" submarine warfare, February, 1916.
      The Battle of Jutland, May 31, 1916.
      Hayes, III, 143-158; 163; 165-166.

F. Stiffening resistance of the Allies.
   1. Attempted co-ordination of Allied plans, military and economic.
   2. The Russian drives on the Styr and the Sereth.
   3. The Italian offensive on the Isonzo: capture of Gorizia, August, 1916.
   4. Anglo-French offensive in the West: Battle of the Somme, July-September, 1916.
   5. Estimate of the relative strength and weaknesses of the belligerents in the fall of 1916.
      Hayes, III, 168-181.

G. Moves for peace.
   1. The Teutonic "peace drive": the proposal of December 12.
   2. Replies of the Allies.

3. Independent peace proposal of the President of the United
    States, December 18; replies of the belligerents.
    Hayes, III, 191-200.

H. The neutral nations and the war.
    1. Economic effects of the war upon the neutrals.
    2. Propaganda and intrigue in neutral nations.
    3. The German submarine campaign and growing irritation
        of non-belligerents.
        The United States and the *Lusitania* and *Arabic* cases.
        Neutral protests against "unrestricted" submarine war-
        fare.
        The United States and the *Sussex* case: diplomatic nego-
        tiations and eventual German repudiation of "ruth-
        lessness."
    4. Causes leading to the belligerency of Portugal, March,
        1916.
        Hayes, III, 162-164.

III. Turn of the Tide: Intervention of the United States.

A. The issue in the United States: peace or war?
    1. Factors contributing to the persistence of American neu-
        trality.
        Geographical isolation.
        Traditional American policies.
        "Isolation" and opposition to "entangling alliances."
        The Monroe Doctrine.
        Devotion to international arbitration.
        "Freedom of the seas."
        Popular attitude toward the causes of the war and to-
        ward the belligerents.
    2. Factors contributing to the eventual participation of the
        United States.
        Economic interests.
        Gradual formulation of an American opinion sympa-
        thetic to the Allies.
        German intrigue and Allied propaganda.
        American agitation for "preparedness."
    3. Formulation of an American program of a just peace.
        Issues of the presidential campaign of 1916.
        President Wilson's peace proposal of December 18, 1916.
        The famous address to the Senate, January 22, 1917.

B. The occasion of American intervention: unrestricted submarine
warfare.
  1. The German declaration of January 31, 1917, announcing
     unrestricted use of the submarine against belligerent
     and neutral vessels alike.
     Reasons for the renewal of unrestricted submarine war-
     fare by Germany.
     The proposal of a "safety lane" for American ships.
  2. Breach of diplomatic relations with Germany, February 3,
     1917.
  3. "Armed neutrality" or war?
  4. The die is cast.
     The "Zimmermann Note."
     "Overt acts."
     The Declaration of War, April 6, 1917.
  5. Influence of the Russian Revolution on public opinion in
     America.

C. The strength of the United States and the cause of the Allies.
  1. Moral effect of the participation of the United States.
  2. Economic resources of the United States: credits, food,
     munitions, shipping.
  3. Military and naval strength of the United States.
     Early adoption of conscription: The Selective Service
     Act.
  4. The problem: speed in economic and military mobilization.
     Hayes, III, 201-224.

IV. Rising Fortunes of the Allies and Final Achievement of Victory.

A. Failure of the German offensive at sea: unrestricted submarine
warfare does not compel the Allies to sue for peace.

B. The campaign of 1917 on the Western Front paves the way for
ultimate victory of the Allies.
  1. The German "strategic retreat" to the Hindenburg Line
     (March, 1917).
  2. Attempts of the Allies to take the pivots of the Hinden-
     burg Line.
     Battle of Arras, April, 1917.
     Second Battle of the Aisne, April, 1917.

3. Warfare of "attrition": Vimy Ridge, Chemin des Dames, Soissons, Verdun, Flanders.
4. Open warfare at Cambrai, November-December, 1917.
5. Summary of gains and losses.
   Hayes, III, 261-281.

C. A serious, but temporary, setback: the defection of Russia.
   1. First phase of the Russian Revolution strengthens the cause of the Allies.*
      Downfall of the Tsardom and the "war for democracy."
      Reaffirmation of the Provisional Government of loyalty to the Allies.
   2. War weariness of the Russian people.
      Tremendous sacrifices previously made in prosecution of the war.
      Economic misery and disorganization.
      Disintegrating forces in the armies.
      Association of the war with imperialist ambitions of the Tsardom.
      German influence and propaganda.
   3. Manifestations of war weariness: moves toward peace.
      The Soviets and the demand for a restatement of war aims: the formula of "self-determination" and "no annexations and no indemnities."
      Kerensky's proposal for an Inter-Allied Conference for the revision of war aims.
      Reactions of the Allies to the Russian proposals.
   4. The abortive Russian offensive of July, 1917.
   5. Failure of the régime of Kerensky.
      Collapse of discipline in the army.
      The Kornilov revolt and other internal dissension.
      War weariness the political stock-in-trade of the Bolsheviki.
   6. The November (1917) Revolution: Dictatorship of the Bolsheviki.
      Responsibility of the Allies for the downfall of Kerensky.
      The Bolsheviki renew the demand for a restatement of war aims.
      Publication of the secret treaties.

* Domestic phases of the Russian Revolution are treated separately; see below, pp. 107-111.

Cessation of the war against Germany: the armistice of December, 1917.

7. Peace negotiations and the Treaty of Brest-Litovsk, March 3, 1918.

8. The isolation and surrender of Rumania: the Treaty of Bucharest, March 7.
   Hayes, III, 225-260.

D. Recovery of Allied prestige in the Near East during 1917.
   1. Maude's campaign in Mesopotamia.
      Creation of the independent Arab sultanate of Hedjaz, in alliance with the Allies.
      Importance of the capture of Bagdad, March, 1917.
   2. Entry of Greece into the war.
      Venizelos and pro-Ally propaganda in Greece.
      Forced abdication of King Constantine, June, 1917.
      The belligerency of Greece, July, 1917, and the strengthening of the Macedonian front.
   3. Allenby's campaign in Palestine: capture of Jerusalem, December, 1917.
   4. Temporary strengthening of the position of the Central Powers: the Italian "debacle" of October-December.
      Hayes, III, 281-287, 293-297.

E. Moves for peace.
   1. War weariness of the European peoples.
      "Defeatism" in Allied countries.
      Weakening morale in the Teutonic nations.
   2. Peace proposals and peace manœuvres prior to the final test of strength.
      Socialist moves for peace.
      The peace note of Pope Benedict XV, August 1, 1917, and replies of the belligerents.
      Lord Lansdowne's plea for a "peace by compromise."
   3. The moral contribution of President Wilson: restatement of the war aims of the Allies in the "Fourteen Points," January, 1918.
      Hayes, III, 287-298.

F. Germany's supreme effort: the offensive of 1918.
   1. The new methods of attack: "storm troops" and "infiltration."
   2. The drive against the British: the Battle of Picardy, March-May.

3. The drive against the French: the Aisne and the Oise, May-June.
4. The drive against the Italians: the Piave, June-July.
5. The final German offensive: the Second Battle of the Marne, July.
   Hayes, III, 299-325.

G. The collapse of the Central Powers and the triumph of the Allies.
   1. Importance of unified command of the Allies.
   2. The Second Battle of the Marne as an Allied victory.
   3. Unsuccessful German resistance on the Western Front.
      The September offensive of the Americans at St. Mihiel.
      The Franco-American offensive on the Meuse and in the Argonne.
      Allied successes in other sectors.
   4. Half-hearted resistance of the Bulgars to the Allied offensive in Macedonia.
   5. The war in Asia Minor and defeat of Turkey.
   6. Internal disorders and the Italian offensive result in the collapse of Austria-Hungary.
      Hayes, III, 326-334, 342-356.

H. The cessation of hostilities, 1918.
   1. The armistice with Bulgaria, September 30.
   2. The armistice with Turkey, October 30.
   3. Austrian pleas for peace and the armistice of November 3.
   4. Negotiations leading to the armistice of November 11 with Germany.
      Hayes, III, 356-364.

J. An aftermath of the War: persistence of Allied military intervention in Russia.
   Hayes, III, 334-342.

K. Summary of the costs of the Great War.
   1. In human life.
   2. In treasure.
      Hayes, III, 388-395.

PART III.   THE PEACE CONFERENCE AND THE SETTLEMENT

I.   Organization and Problems of the Conference.

A.   Colossal task of the Peace Conference.

B.   Conflicting theories as to the basic principles of a just peace.
1.   Advocates of the imposition upon the Central Powers of a punitive peace.
2.   Defenders of the sacredness and inviolability of the "secret treaties."
3.   The Russian formula of peace "without annexations and indemnities."
4.   Demands for "reparation,"—economic and political.
5.   The American program: the Fourteen Points.
6.   Consideration of these conflicting programs complicated by an increase of nationalistic agitation which accompanied the flush of victory.

C.   Attempts to reconcile conflicting aims and policies of the Allied powers.
1.   Exclusion of the Central Powers from the preliminary conference in order to avoid emphasis upon these conflicts of interests.
2.   The decision in favor of secret diplomacy.
3.   Fundamental alterations in the American program because of concessions to the special interests of other Allied powers.
Great Britain and the "freedom of the seas."
France and the proposed defensive alliance with Great Britain and the United States.
Japan and the question of Shantung.
4.   Insistence of President Wilson upon incorporation in the treaties of the Covenant of the League of Nations.

D.   Personnel and organization of the Conference.
1.   Representation and representatives of the Allied nations.
2.   Importance of the work of the Committees and the cooperation of "experts."

3. The controlling force of the Conference: the Supreme Council (Council of Ten; then Council of Five; finally Council of Four).

Hayes, III, 365-371. **C. H. Haskins & R. H. Lord,** *Some Problems of the Peace Conference* (Cambridge, 1920), Chap. I. **E. R. Turner,** *Europe, 1789-1920* (New York, 1920), 576-585.

II. General Character of the Settlement.

A. The treaties which constitute the settlement.
   1. The Treaty of Versailles with Germany, June, 1919.
   2. The Treaty of St. Germain with Austria, September, 1919.
   3. The Treaty of Neuilly with Bulgaria, November, 1919.
   4. The Treaty of the Trianon with Hungary, June, 1920.
   5. The Treaty of Sèvres with Turkey, August, 1920.

B. Punitive measures against the Central Powers.
   1. Military and naval.
   2. Economic: indemnities and reparations.
   3. Political: cessions of territory and loss of colonies.

C. Territorial readjustments in Europe.
   1. Territorial annexations of members of the Entente coalition.
   2. Territories the nationality of which has been or is to be fixed by plebiscite.
   3. New national states.
      The Republic of Poland and the free city of Danzig.
      The Republic of Czechoslovakia.
      Jugoslavia (Kingdom of the Serbs, Croats, and Slovenes).
      The Baltic republics: Finland, Esthonia, Latvia, Lithuania.
      The Republic of Hungary.
      The Ukrainian Republic.
      Albania.
   4. Expulsion of the Turks from Europe.

D. Territorial readjustments outside of Europe.
   1. Disposition of the German colonies: the mandatary system.
   2. The dismemberment of Turkey.
      Neutral zone of the Straits.
      The Greek mandate in Smyrna.

British mandates in Palestine and Mesopotamia.

The French mandate in Syria.

The independent Armenian, Georgian, and Azerbaijan republics.

The independent Kingdom of the Hedjaz.

3. Cession to Japan of the German rights in Shantung.

E. The Labor Convention an integral part of the settlement.
   1. Provision for an annual International Labor Conference.
   2. Definitions of minimum industrial standards.

F. Other economic clauses of the treaties.
   1. Regulations regarding shipping, tariffs, finance.
   2. Control of ports, waterways, railways.

G. Covenant of the League of Nations.
   1. Membership in the League.
   2. Government of the League: the Council; the Assembly; the Secretariat.
   3. Measures toward the limitation of armaments and the prevention of war.
   4. Measures in the interest of international economic and social welfare.
   5. The mandatary system under the League.
      Hayes, III, 373-388. **E. R. Turner,** *Europe, 1789-1920,* 585-597.
      Map Study Number Fourteen.

III.   The Treaties in Force.

A. The exchange of ratifications.

B. Dissent from the settlement and its principles.
   1. Refusal of China to sign the Treaty of Versailles.
   2. American dissatisfaction with the Treaty of Versailles.
      The Senate reservations.
      Opposition to the League.
      Opposition to the Treaty.
   3. Poland's war on Russia a denial of the jurisdiction of the Conference in delimitation of the Russo-Polish boundary.
   4. The Turkish nationalists and armed rebellion against enforcement of the Treaty of Sèvres.
   5. The venture of D'Annunzio in Fiume, September, 1919,-December, 1920.

C. Modifications of the settlement by force of circumstances.
  1. The question of German disarmament.
  2. The question of determining the German indemnity.

D. The League of Nations in operation.
  1. Establishment of the permanent Secretariat at Geneva.
  2. Administrative and executive activities of the Council.
  3. First meeting of the Assembly of the League, November-December, 1920.
    Conflicts of authority between Assembly and Council.
    Question of amendments to the Covenant; withdrawal of Argentina.
    Failure to agree on a program for disarmament.
    Admission of Austria and Bulgaria to membership in the League.
      Hayes, III, 373; 381-383; 385-386; 424-427. **Turner,** *Europe, 1789-1920,* 592.

PART IV. NATIONALISM AND REPUBLICANISM DURING THE WAR AND AFTER

I. The Russian Revolution.

A. Imperial Russia in the Great War.
  1. Internal dissension submerged in national patriotism with outbreak of war.
    Pan-Slavism and the popularity of the war.
    Popular participation in prosecution of the war: the War Industries Committee, All-Russian Union of Zemstvos, etc.
    Unprecedented opportunity of the Tsardom to achieve national solidarity and loyalty through moderate reforms.
  2. The autocracy misreads the signs of the times: the policy of reaction.
    Emptiness of the promise of autonomy to the Poles (August, 1914); effect upon loyalty of other dissentient nationalities.
    Suppression of opposition press and prosecution of liberals.
    Reactionary ministers: Stürmer, Trepov, Protopopov, Soukhomlinov.

>   Pro-German influences in the government.
>   Rasputin and the Tsarina.
> 3. The revival of discontent.
>   Military defeat discredits the autocracy.
>   The reform program of the Duma of 1915.
>   Appalling casualties in the Russian armies and the be-
>   ginnings of war-weariness.
>   Disorganization of transportation and industry.
>   Economic misery and industrial discontent.
> 4. The issue of making Russia safe for democracy over-
>   shadows the issue of "making the world safe for
>   democracy."
>   **Hayes, III,** 53-55; 107-112; 194; 225-227.

B. The downfall of the autocracy: the March (1917) Revolution.
> 1. Factors in the success of the March Revolution.
>   Strikes, riots, demonstrations of the workmen of Pet-
>   rograd.
>   Refusal of the Duma to be prorogued (March 11).
>   Support of the Revolution by the army.
> 2. Abdication of the Tsar, March 15, 1917.
>   **Hayes, III,** 227-229; **Ogg,** 741-743.

C. First phase of the Revolution, March-July, 1917: the moderate
   bourgeois Provisional Government of Prince Lvov.
> 1. The coalition ministry: influence of Milyukov and
>   Kerensky.
> 2. Bourgeois reforms of the Provisional Government.
> 3. The crucial question of war aims.
> 4. Reconstruction of the ministry, May, 1917.
>   Decreased representation of Constitutional Democrats
>   and Octobrists.
>   Increased representation of Socialist Revolutionaries;
>   advent to the ministry of representatives of the
>   Social Democrats.
> 5. Opposition to the Provisional Government.
>   Tsarists and reactionaries.
>   Conservative bourgeoisie.
>   Nationalist minorities.
>   Pro-Germans and German propaganda.
>   Radicals.
>   Socialist Revolutionaries.
>   Social Democrats.

The Menshiviki.

The Bolsheviki: Lenin and Trotsky.

6. Failure of the July offensive and the downfall of the Lvov ministry.

Hayes, III, 229-244.

D. Second phase of the Revolution, July-November, 1917: the moderate Socialist régime of Kerensky.

1. Premature uprising of the Bolsheviki (July, 1917) and the dictatorship of Kerensky.
2. Kornilov's attempt to establish a military dictatorship.
3. Refusal of the Allies to co-operate with Kerensky in a restatement of war aims.

Hayes, III, 244-247.

E. Third phase of the Revolution, November, 1917: dictatorship of the Bolsheviki.

1. The Bolshevist *coup d'état* of November 7, 1917.
2. Fundamental characteristics of the Bolshevist régime.

A government originating in force and maintained by force.

A dictatorship maintained by a class in the interest of a class.

A repudiation of political democracy.

Dissolution of the National Constituent Assembly, January, 1918.

Limitation of the suffrage to "producers."

Influence of Tsarist schooling on political methods of the Bolsheviki.

3. The Constitution of the "Russian Socialist Federated Soviet Republic."

A series of declarations and decrees, ratified by the Fifth All-Russian Congress of Soviets, July, 1918.

"Declaration of the Rights of the Toiling and Exploited People."

The economic and social revolution decreed by the Constitution.

Displacement of representation on a geographical basis by representation on an occupational basis.

The structure of Government.

The All-Russian Congress.

The All-Russian Executive Committee.

The Council of People's Commissars.

   4. Foreign relations of the Bolshevist government.

      Treaty of Brest-Litovsk.

      Allied intervention in Russia: its pretexts and its purposes.

      Russia and the Peace Conference.

      Persistence of French intervention: the "Cordon Sanitaire."

      The War with Poland.

   5. Failure of counter-revolution in Russia.

      Allied support of counter-revolutionary ventures.

      Failure of Kolchak, Denikin, Yudenitch, and Wrangel.

   6. The economic and social revolution under the Bolsheviki.

      The goal of the Bolsheviki: the complete destruction of bourgeois society.

      Significant revolutionary measures.

         Abolition of private property; communism.

         Nationalization of land and of industries in the interests of the peasants and workers respectively.

         Repudiation of the national debt.

         Disestablishment of the Church and secularization of education.

         Universal compulsory labor: "He shall not eat who does not work."

      Modification of Bolshevist theories in practice.

      Hayes, III, 247-255, 255-260; **Ogg,** 743-754.

F. The Russian Revolution and the disintegration of the Russian Empire.

   1. The independence of Poland.

      The independent "Kingdom of Poland," a German creature, November, 1916.

      Pilsudski and the Committee of National Defense.

      The independence of Poland a war aim of the Allies.

      Proclamation of the Polish People's Republic, November 6, 1918.

      Recognition of the claims of Poland by the Peace Conference.

   2. The Ukrainian People's Republic.

      Proclamation of the independence of the "Little Russians," November, 1917.

      Representation at the Peace Conference of Brest-Litovsk.

Ukrainia a Socialist Republic.
3. Independence of the Baltic states.
   The Republic of Finland.
   The republics of Lithuania, Latvia, and Esthonia.
4. The Transcaucasian republics of Georgia and Azerbaijan.
5. Secessionist movements in South Russia.
6. The nebulous Republic of Siberia, under Japanese influence.
   Hayes, III, 195-196; 237-238; 255-256; 297-298; 359; 374-376.

II. The Republican Revolution in Germany.

A. National solidarity in Germany with the outbreak of the war.

B. The war-time demand for political reform.
   1. The cabinet crises of 1917.
      Effects of the Russian Revolution and the intervention of the United States in the war.
      Fall of the Bethmann-Hollweg ministry, July, 1917.
      The Chancellorship of George Michaelis, July-October, 1917.
      Significance of the appointment as Chancellor of Count Hertling.
   2. Junker reaction with the military victories of the spring of 1918.
   3. Renewal of the demand for reform in the summer of 1918.
      Proposed re-apportionment of representation in the Reichstag.
      Resignation of Hertling and appointment of the coalition ministry of Prince Maximilian, September 30, 1918.
   4. Tardy reforms of the Imperial Government.
      Nominal responsibility of the Chancellor to the Reichstag.
      Constitutional amendment depriving Emperor of the power to make war without consent of Reichstag and Bundesrat.
   5. Announcement of a scheme of electoral reform in Prussia.
      Hayes, III, 166, 266-269, 330-331; Ogg, 706-710.

C. The republican revolution of November, 1918.
   1. The collapse of monarchical institutions.

Proclamation of the Bavarian republic, November 8.

Establishment of the Imperial Regency, with Ebert as Chancellor, November 9.

Complete triumph of republicanism throughout Germany.

Abdication of the Kaiser, November 28, and of the Crown Prince, December 1.

2. Difficulties of the Ebert Government.

Economic and political disorganization.

Opponents of the Revolution.

Reactionaries: Junkers, pan-Germans, royalists.

Extreme radicals: the Spartacans.

Hayes, III, 356-363; **Ogg,** 710-716.

D. The National Constituent Assembly and its work, February, 1919-July, 1919.

1. The Assembly chosen by universal, direct, secret suffrage of both men and women.

2. Parties in the Assembly (in order of numerical **represen-**tation).

Majority Socialists.

Christian People's Party (Catholic Center).

German Democratic Party (Progressives).

National People's Party (Conservatives).

Independent Socialists.

People's Party (National Liberals).

3. Adoption of a provisional constitution, with Ebert **as** Provisional President.

4. The Constitution of the German Republic, adopted July 31, 1919.

Bill of Rights.

Statement of the social and economic program of the Republic.

Limitations on the powers of the states.

Requirement that every state must have a republican government.

Restrictions on the governmental powers of **the** states.

The Reichstag, or National Assembly.

Membership, manner of election, and powers.

The Reichsrat, or National Council.

Membership and powers.

The Executive: the President and the Cabinet.

The Judiciary.

Provisions regarding use of initiative, referendum, and recall.

Comparison of the German Constitution with the constitutions of the United States and of Switzerland.
Hayes, III, 363-364; **Ogg,** 717-732.

E. The German Republic on trial.
  1. The royalist counter-revolution of March, 1920.
     Leaders of the militarist-royalist *coup:* von Kapp and von Lüttwitz.
     The general strike and failure of the counter-revolution.
  2. Party alignments in 1920.
  3. The elections of June, 1920.
     Losses of the Government *bloc:* Majority Socialists, Democratic Party, and Christian People's Party.
     Gains of the extremists.
     Radicals: Independent Socialists and Communists.
     Reactionaries: National People's Party (Conservatives) and German People's Party (National Liberals).
  4. The chancellorship of Konstantin Fehrenbach (Centrist).
     The coalition ministry.
  5. Colossal nature of the economic and social problems of the Republic.
     Ogg, 732-736.

III. The Disintegration of the Austrian Empire.

A. The war and the revival of nationalist agitation in the Dual Monarchy.
  1. Meeting of the Reichsrat in 1917 prorogued because of nationalist disturbances.
  2. Propaganda for Czech and Polish independence.
  3. The Jugoslavs and the Declaration of Corfu, July, 1917.
     Hayes, III, 263-266.

B. Military defeat and the collapse of the Austrian Empire.
  1. Formation of the Republic of Czechoslovakia.
     Declaration of independence, October, 1918.
     The Czechoslovak National Assembly, November, 1918.
  2. The United Kingdom of Serbs, Croats, and Slovenes (Jugoslavia).
     The Agram Convention and the choice of King Peter

of Serbia as monarch and of Prince Alexander as
regent.

Problems of Jugoslavia: boundary disputes with Italy.

3. The Hungarian Republic.

Establishment of Hungarian independence, October, 1918.

Proclamation of the Republic, November, 1918.

The Communist régime of Bela Kun, March-July, 1919.

The National Assembly and its problems.

4. The Republic of German Austria.

Proclamation of the Republic by the National Assembly,
November 13, 1918.

Desire of German Austria to be united with Germany
frustrated by the Peace Conference.

Election of the National Constituent Assembly, February, 1919.

Democratic character of the suffrage.

Predominance of Social Democrats and Christian
Socialists.

Dr. Karl Renner as chancellor.

Austria overwhelmed by economic distress, December,
1920.

Hayes, III, 348-356; 383; 386-387.

IV. The British Empire and the War.

A. Nationalist and Home Rule agitation in India.

1. Indian loyalty to Great Britain during the war.
2. Reasons for the revival of discontent in India.

Economic distress and labor disturbances.

Famine and the influenza epidemic.

Illiteracy and poverty.

Subordination of Indian economic and political interests
to those of Great Britain.

Mohammedan unrest over defeat and proposed dismemberment of Turkey.

3. Organization of Nationalist and Home Rule agitation.

The Indian National Congress.

All India Moslem League.

National Home Rule League.

Labor unions.

Passive Resistance League.

4. Repressive measures of the British government.

Defence of India Act: the censorship; government espionage; suppression of "sedition."

Rowlatt Acts: emergency acts granting to the military and police extraordinary powers of search, arrest, and punishment (March, 1919).

Ruthless military suppression of agitation: the "Amritsar Massacre," April, 1919.

5. The Montagu-Chelmsford Report, August, 1917.

Principle advocated by the report: gradual extension of home rule in India.

Dissatisfaction of the Nationalists.

6. The Government of India Act, December, 1919.

Increased local self-government.

Changes in the central government: the bicameral Indian Legislature.

Reform of the civil service.

Other measures looking toward eventual home rule for India.

Hayes, 66; **Cross,** 900-905.

B. Egyptian revolt against the Protectorate.

1. Egyptian grievances against the British protectorate.

Forced recruiting.

Suspension of the Egyptian Assembly during the war.

Censorship of the news and suppression of Nationalist opinions.

Exclusion of native newspapers and political discussions from the schools.

Arrest and deportation of Egyptian "representatives" at the Peace Conference.

2. The "Young Egyptians" and the persistence of Nationalist agitation.

3. Field Marshal Viscount Allenby as British High Commissioner: the suppression of disorder (1919).

4. The Milner Mission to Egypt and its report.

Hostile attitude shown toward the Mission by the Egyptians.

Its report submitted December, 1920: nature of the recommendations.

Recognition of the independence of Egypt.

Autonomous executive, legislative, and judicial departments.

British protection against foreign invasion.
Cross, 896-897.

C. The republican movement in Ireland.
    1. Review of the Irish situation in August, 1914.
        The Home Rule Bill of 1914.
        Resistance of the Ulsterites and the division of Ireland
        into two armed camps.
        Suspension of the Home Rule Bill at the outbreak of the
        war.
        Temporary submersion of Irish factional quarrels in
        common loyalty to the British cause.
    2. Factors in the revival of discontent in Ireland, 1915-1916.
        Continued suspension of the Home Rule Bill.
        Recruiting in Ireland for the British Expeditionary
        Forces.
        War taxes and other economic grievances.
        Aggressive republican propaganda.
            Growth of Sinn Fein.
            The Gaelic League.
            James Larkin and the development of radical labor
            organizations.
    3. The abortive Sinn Fein rebellion of 1916.
        Sir Roger Casement and the conspiracy with Germany.
        Proclamation of the "republic" in Dublin, April, 1916.
        British suppression of the revolt by military force.
        The bitter aftermath: execution of the leaders; imprison-
        ment of hundreds; establishment of martial law.
    4. The Irish Convention, July, 1917-April, 1918.
        A constituent assembly convened by the British Govern-
        ment.
        Refusal of the Sinn Fein to send delegates.
        Obstructionist policies of the Unionists.
        Report of the Convention, recommending Dominion plan
        of government for Ireland, rejected by the Govern-
        ment.
    5. Attempted application of conscription to Ireland, April,
        1918.
        Opposition of all classes in Ireland: British Government
        compelled to abandon conscription.
        Increased bitterness between England and Ireland.

Appointment of Field Marshal Viscount French as Lord
Lieutenant.
6. Growth of the republican movement.
Overwhelming victory of Sinn Fein in the elections of
December, 1918.
7. "The Irish Republic."
Proclaimed at Dublin, January 21, 1919.
Structure of the Republic: President de Valera and Dail
Eireann.
The Irish Republican Army.
Attempted representation of Ireland at the Peace Con-
ference.
8. Attempted suppression of the Republic.
Suppression of the Irish Parliament, September, 1919.
Sinn Fein victories in municipal elections of January,
1920.
Arrest of Sinn Fein municipal officials: the case of
Terence MacSwiney.
The British Government's Home Rule Bill of 1920.
9. The Reign of Terror in Ireland.
Hayes, III, 158-161; 262-263; 310-312; 387; **Cross,**
882-890.

D. The War and attempts at imperial co-operation.
1. Rôle of the self-governing colonies in the war.
2. The Imperial War Conference and the Imperial War
Cabinet, 1917-1918.
3. Proposals for a permanent Imperial Cabinet and other
measures of imperial co-operation, political and
economic.
Cross, 891-895; 905-907.

**PART V. OTHER POLITICAL AND SOCIAL DEVELOPMENTS OF
WAR-TIME**

I. The Growth of Political Democracy.

A. Electoral reform and extension of the suffrage.
1. Representation of the People Act of 1918 in Great
Britain.

Redistribution of seats in the interest of proportional representation.

Reform of electoral procedure.

Radical extension of the franchise, including restricted suffrage for women.

2. The Electoral Reform Bill of 1919 in France.
3. Plural voting abolished in Belgium, 1919.
4. Political reform in Rumania: universal suffrage substituted for the Prussian three-class system.
5. Ratification of the Eighteenth Amendment to the Constitution of the United States, enfranchising women (August, 1920).
6. General recognition of the principle of universal, direct, secret suffrage, without distinction because of sex, in new republics on the Continent.

B. The growth of democracy accompanied, however, by the growth of political intolerance.
1. Censorship and espionage laws.
2. Violation of constitutional guarantees of individual liberties.
3. Intolerance of minorities.
4. Question of the permanence of political intolerance.
   Hayes, III, 403-405; **Cross,** 880-881.

II. The Growth of Industrial Democracy.

A. The program of the British Labor Party during the war and after.
1. Support of the war by British labor and participation in the Coalition Government by representatives of the British Labor Party.
2. War aims of the British Labor Party.
3. The Party's program of reconstruction: "Labor and the New Social Order."
4. Program of the Labor Party in the elections of December, 1918.

B. The movement toward industrial democracy in Great Britain.
1. Trade unionism and the war: influence of the "shop stewards."
2. The Triple Alliance of labor and the growing demand for

nationalization of industry. Significant report of
the Coal Commission of 1920.
3. The growth of Gild Socialism.
4. The "Whitley Council" idea.
5. The permanent National Industrial Conference.

C. Italy's interesting experiment in industrial democracy.
   1. The Italian Metal Workers' Federation secures participation in the management of their industry.
The lockout of September, 1920, in Lombardy.
Seizure of plants by the workers.
Arbitration by Premier Giolitti results in recognition by
employers of the right of the workers to a share in
management.
The agreement of October, 1920, accepting Premier
Giolitti's plan.
   2. The Government proposal of 1921 to extend workers'
participation in control to other industries.
   3. Growth of syndicalism and communism in Italy.

D. Growth in number and power of labor organizations in other
continental countries.

E. The vogue of Marxian Socialism in continental Europe.
        Hayes, III, 21-22; 406-408; **Cross,** 876-879; 881-882;
        Cheyney, 351-368.

III. Intellectual Progress.

A. Great development of experimental science.
   1. Miscellaneous war inventions possible of adaptation to
peaceful purposes: progress in aeronautics; in chem-
istry; wireless telephony, etc.
   2. The great advance of medical science.

B. Increased interest in the social sciences: history and international relations, economics, government, sociology.

C. The war and educational progress.
   1. General popular appreciation of the national importance of
education.
   2. Far-reaching British Education Bill of 1918.
Provisions regarding the employment of children.
Establishment of continuation schools.

Provisions regarding medical care, playgrounds, physical training, etc.

Vocational schools and schools for defectives.

Higher salaries for teachers.

Hayes, III, 408-410; **Cross,** 879-880.

IV. The War and Religion.

A. Co-operation of creeds, churches, religions in common national service.

B. The political and ecclesiastical position of the Catholic Church during the war and after.

Hayes, III, 410-411.

Appendix I.

STUDYING AND NOTE-TAKING.

How to Study.

Proper historical study involves, first, visualization; second, memorizing; third, discrimination. The Syllabus is designed to guide the student in each of these essential processes. The map studies are intended to assist him in forming a mental picture of the countries of which he reads in the text; the relative importance of topics and dates is indicated in order that he may concentrate his memory upon essentials; the topical outline is a guide in the evaluation and co-ordination of text material. All study is valueless without strict mental concentration and discipline. No plan ought to be or, indeed, can be devised as a substitute for these fundamentals of concentration and discipline; the suggestions here offered as to methods of approach, therefore, should not be considered as designed to encourage short-cuts to historical knowledge, but, rather, to arouse *interest* through *thoroughness*.

Suppose, for purposes of illustrating our plan of study, that the topic for study and discussion is "Agriculture in the sixteenth century" (Book I, sub-topic II, A). The student should first familiarize himself thoroughly with the sub-topics in the indicated section of the Syllabus. Then he should spread out before him, side by side, the text-book and the atlas. As he studies the text-book narrative (**Hayes, I,** pp. 28-36) he should retain in mind the sub-topics of the Syllabus as a guide in co-ordinating the details of the text; also he should visualize the physical features of a mediæval manor as illustrated in the atlas (**Shepherd,** p. 104, or **Muir,** diagram xxvi). Next he should fill in gaps between Syllabus, text-book, and atlas by reading the suggested pages in **Cheyney** or whatever other collateral reading may be decided upon. Notes should then be taken in the manner described in the following paragraph.[1] Finally, to test his knowledge, he should close his books, transform the statements of

[1] Should a map study be required with an assignment, it may be prepared after the note-book work has been completed.

the Syllabus into questions, and endeavor to give himself clear and complete answers to the questions asked. As final suggestions, the student should keep constantly in mind the following: 1. To develop an intimate acquaintance with his atlas, which should be a constant companion during his hours of historical study. 2. To lay up a generous store of historical facts by constant exercise of his memory; dates in the Syllabus, for example, should be memorized. 3. To be critical in his study,—that is, to not only learn facts, but to inquire as to their causal relations; to not only learn the characteristics of persons and peoples, but to acquire a sympathetic appreciation of their motives and their ideals, their strength and their weaknesses.

The Note Book.

The purpose of all note-taking should be to insure a habit of logical arrangement of facts gained from the printed page. A complete note-book, properly compiled, will be of inestimable value in the proper appreciation of the study of history and should prove to be a source of considerable interest to the conscientious student. In summarizing text material the student is expected to condense into the fewest words possible the important facts or suggestions, arranging them topically according to the Syllabus with sub-topics in outline form to show the relation of one to another. For purposes of illustrating the method of outlining, the student may turn again to the topic "Agriculture in the sixteenth century," and to **Hayes I,** 28-36, and notice how the following summary corresponds:

II.   Social and Economic Institutions of the Century.

A.   Agriculture.
  1.   Predominance of agriculture over other occupations, etc.
    a.   Wealth in land rather than in stocks and bonds.
    b.   Towns as yet small and few.
    c.   Uniformity of agricultural conditions throughout Europe.
  2.   Division of the agricultural population into two classes, etc.
    a.   The proprietors of the land: the landed aristocracy.
        Owed duties to king or fellow-noblemen.
        Supported by peasants living on estates, called "manors."
        Wealth and honors.

Reasons for preëminence of the nobility: former duties of military protection of peasantry; now continued by inheritance to enjoy financial privileges and social prestige.

b. The workers of the land: the peasantry.

Serfs.

Different from slaves, hired men, tenant-farmers.

Free to work for self part time; no wages; "attached to soil."

Obligations to lord of the manor: work two or three days weekly, "boon days," dues "in kind," "heriot," etc.

Free tenants.

Increasing numbers.

Regular dues owed to lord; usually not obliged to work two or three days weekly for him, however; free to move away from manor.

Hired laborers.

Workers for wages on the lord's land (demesne).

Métayers (France); Stock-and-land lessees (England).

Farmers "on shares."

3. Decline of feudalism and serfdom in western Europe.

 a. Serfdom unprofitable to the lord, galling to the serf.

 b. In England, "enclosures" for sheep-raising.

 c. Survival of serfdom in eastern Europe.

4. The manor and the "three field" system of agriculture.

 a. Persistence after decline of serfdom.

 b. Physical features of the manor: "commons" of pasture and woodland; "strips" in open fields, etc.

 c. Inefficiency.

Time wasted in working separated strips.

Small yield per acre.

Crude implements.

Obstacles to effective breeding of cattle.

5. Life in the country, etc.

 a. Dark side: poverty, cold, poor diet, disease, famine, etc.

 b. Bright side: contrast with present-day tenements and factories; occasional luxuries, etc.

 c. Isolation, self-sufficiency, and conservatism.

B. Commerce and industry before the commercial revolution.

This illustration is simply a topical outline of the text-book in the order indicated in the Syllabus. If the student does supplementary reading, he should amplify the outline to include significant facts gained from that source.

The student may vary this plan according to the dictates of his ingenuity. Except under the guidance of an instructor, however, the outline form should not be dispensed with or seriously modified. Appropriate provision should be made for the inclusion in the note-book of salient points of class discussions; for example, left-hand pages of the note-book may be specifically reserved for appropriate memoranda of the instructor's informal lectures or other classroom work. Newspaper articles of special interest and appropriate photographs may be incorporated in the note-book if desired. Such points of organization and of amplification, however, are left to the decision of the individual student and instructor.

It would be inadvisable indeed to lay down these rules for the note-book as ironbound and unchangeable. As a matter of fact, the instructor probably will find it desirable to discontinue the formal exercise of note-taking and the periodical examination of note-books if, in his opinion, several weeks of the work have impressed upon the student the desirability of keeping a record of the course and have trained him in the habit of evaluating and co-ordinating his material. In this, as in other respects, the course of study here offered is intended to be elastic and suggestive rather than rigid and authoritative.

Appendix II.

MAP STUDIES.

The Purpose of Map Studies.

"Man has been so noisy about the way he has 'conquered Nature,' and Nature has been so silent in her persistent influence over men, that the geographic factor in the equation of human development has been overlooked."[1]

Although this statement is, in large measure, still true, there has been a gradually growing appreciation of the inseparable relationship of historical facts and geographical facts. The influence of natural environment upon man and upon the institutions of man's creation is now a subject of a group of the social sciences,—such as anthropology, ethnology, sociology. It is no less a fundamental factor in the study of history, for "man can no more be scientifically studied apart from the ground which he tills, or the lands over which he travels, or the sea over which he trades, than the polar bear or desert cactus can be understood apart from its habitat."[2] Industry is limited by proximity to fuel or water-power; agriculture thrives where plains and valleys are watered by slow-flowing rivers, not where turbulent streams force their way through ravines and canyons; the development of ocean-going commerce is dependent upon deep-water harbors. The influence of geography upon political history is no less important. Poland was handicapped in the age-long struggle for national unity and independence by the absence of "natural boundaries." The accident of geographical situation made Belgium a martyr to the German invasion of France in 1914; the Alps provide at least one explanation why Switzerland did not suffer a similar fate. No virtue or vice of the individual Belgian or Swiss could alter those fundamental facts and his relationship to them.

The influence of natural environment upon man should not com-

---

[1] E. C. Semple, *Influence of Geographic Environment* (New York, 1911), p. 2.
[2] *Ibid.*

125

pletely overshadow, however, the influence of man upon his natural environment. Man has removed mountains by tunneling through them; he has turned deserts into gardens by irrigation; he has cut continents in two by the construction of canals; he has harnessed the streams to do his will. Time and distance shrink before the instruments of man's creation,—the ocean greyhound, the locomotive, the airplane. In this struggle against the forces of nature the strength and weaknesses of men and of nations are clearly revealed. The story of man cannot be told apart from the story of that struggle.

The following studies in geography are designed to assist the student in grasping essential facts of modern history by making graphic the statements of the printed page, by suggesting interpretations of the facts there recorded, and by affording a vivid picture of the countries of which the history is being studied. The studies are so coördinated with the text assignments that conscientious and thoughtful preparation of the maps in connection with the suggested readings should enable the student to *see* countries and movements grow. If the map work degenerates into mere copying from an atlas, it is a waste of time which could be better employed. Intelligence and imagination invested in the work, however, will bring large returns. It is of the utmost importance to realize that in the study of history the questions *Where?* and *Why?* are as fundamental as the questions *When?* and *Who?*

General Directions.

1. *Clearness* and *neatness* are almost essential to *accuracy*. These qualities can be attained only if each map study is carefully planned in advance. Planning will involve: (a) previous mastery of the relevant text assignment; (b) careful reading of the directions for the map study; (c) the selection of a color scheme. For coloring, inks of different tints, water-colors, or colored pencils may be used; in using pencils and crayons, all lettering should be done and all boundary lines drawn before the color is applied.

2. If possible, map-work should be done by daylight, as colors in the atlas are not readily distinguishable under artificial light.

3. Blunders in elementary historical knowledge are unpardonable. To assure accuracy in his study the student will find it necessary to refer constantly to the text and occasionally to other reference works, such as the Encyclopædia Britannica. Indexes in the text and in the atlases should be utilized habitually.

4. Because of the reduced scale of the outline maps, the wandering of a quarter of an inch may mean an actual error of fifty miles or more. Such an error is serious, and the more so when one is dealing with populous European countries. In the drawing of boundaries the McKinley Outline Maps are not to be followed as trustworthy guides; usually they represent the boundaries of 1905, not of the period with which the map study deals.

5. Lettering should be done neatly and plainly. Place-names italicized in the directions should be located upon the map; when a map is small or detailed, places may be indicated by initials or numbers, explained in a key sheet. Each map study should be accompanied by such a key sheet, in which is given an explanation of the color-scheme, definitions of terms, answers to questions, and other relevant data.

In all probability the fourteen map studies outlined below will be found more than can be conveniently incorporated in the average college course in history. The instructor will have his own ideas regarding the relative importance of the different topics of modern history; therefore, a comparatively large number of map studies have been suggested, leaving the definite choice to the individual instructor or student. It should be pointed out, furthermore, that certain of the map studies may be assigned in part only, as a glance at Map Study Number Five will indicate.

Map Study Number One.

EUROPE IN THE YEAR 1500.

Text: **Hayes I,** 3-23.
Atlas: **Muir. Hayes I,** 3.
McKinley Outline Map No. 101a.

This study is the foundation upon which all subsequent map studies will have to be constructed. Properly done, it will provide the student with a vivid picture of the physical characteristics of the continent of Europe and of its political divisions in the year 1500. Satisfactory progress hardly can be made in the subsequent work unless this study has been mastered thoroughly.

Physical.

Referring to **Muir,** plate 1, note the physical characteristics of Europe. Observe how the land slopes to the north, the whole northern part of Europe from the *Pyrenees*[1] to the *Ural Mountains* forming one great plain. Locate the *Alps, Vosges, Jura, Apennines, Carpathian, Caucasus,* and *Balkan Mountains.* (Use index in **Muir** to locate such of these as are not shown on plate 1.) Note that the Pyrenees are difficult to cross, and that Spain is left in comparative isolation. The Alps, it will be noticed, are higher, but they are cut by a number of passes which render much less difficult communication between Italy and the Germanies. Locate from **Muir,** plate 21b, three important Alpine passes and name them in your key sheet. Indicate on your map the more important rivers of Europe. In what direction do the majority of these rivers flow? Note in your following study of the political divisions of Europe those states which possess "natural boundaries," —such as mountains and rivers—and those which do not.

[1] In this and in subsequent map studies, all places italicized should be indicated on the outline map. Questions should be answered in the key unless the answer is clearly shown on your map.

129

Political.

England: Show the political divisions of the British Isles. Locate the *Pale, Scottish Highlands* and *Lowlands.* Indicate possessions of England outside the British Isles. (Consult **Hayes I,** 3-6; **Muir,** plates 31, 40a, 42a, 15b.)

France: Only slowly did France become a unified state. For centuries preceding 1500 there had been a constant struggle between the king and his turbulent vassals; and although the latter had now been brought into nominal subjection to the crown, we shall still hear much of their quarrels. Under Louis XI (1461-1483) territorial consolidation of the realm had been largely achieved. After reading **Hayes I,** 6-7, and referring to **Muir,** plate 15b, indicate the lands secured by the Angevin inheritance and those obtained by the marriage with Anne of Brittany. Show the lands secured by Louis upon the death of his powerful vassal, Charles the Bold, duke of Burgundy. What other lands were held by powerful vassals of the king,—such as the houses of Orleans, Bourbon, and Navarre?

Iberian Peninsula: Glance at **Muir,** plate 19, and visualize the physical characteristics of the Iberian Peninsula. Does the nature of the country suggest any difficulties in the way of a united Spanish kingdom, centrally administered? After reading **Hayes I,** 7-9, and referring to **Muir,** plate 18d, indicate the political divisions of the Peninsula. Were the Pyrenees the exact boundary between Spain and France in the year 1500? Note the position of *Navarre* and *Roussillon.* What European possessions outside the Iberian Peninsula had the Spanish kingdoms in the year 1500? Indicate these lands on your map (**Muir,** plate 8).

The Germanies: (Read **Hayes I,** 10-14; **Muir,** plate 8). The Germanies in 1500 consisted of a conglomeration of hundreds of states,—kingdoms, duchies, principalities, counties, free imperial cities, and ecclesiastical territories—each jealous of its freedom. A loose and ineffective union existed under the glorified title of the Holy Roman Empire; referring to **Hayes I,** map opposite p. 3, indicate on your map the boundary of the Empire. As among the chief of the states in the Germanies, indicate *Bavaria,* the *Upper* and *Lower Palatinate, Saxony, Brandenburg.* Then there are the extensive possessions of the powerful Habsburg family, which will be considered in greater detail in a subsequent map study. For the present it will be sufficient to locate some of their most important lands: *Austria, Styria, Carinthia, Carniola, Tyrol.* Important ecclesiastical territories are the Archbishoprics of *Mainz* (Mayence), *Trier* (Trèves), *Köln* (Cologne), and *Magdeburg.* Of the host of city-states, the following should be indicated on your map: *Augsburg, Hamburg, Lübeck.* The independence of the *Swiss Cantons* from the Empire has been practically established.

The Italian Peninsula: Italy in 1500 is merely a "geographical expression." In the north are powerful city states:—*Venice,* one of the strongest states in Europe, securing immense wealth from its commerce and controlling *Dalmatia, Crete,* and some of the *Ionian* and *Ægean* Islands; *Genoa,* the commercial rival of Venice, holding sovereignty over *Corsica; Milan,* temporarily under the control of the French king; *Florence,* the center of a noteworthy literary and artistic life. In the northwest will be found the weak, but growing, state of *Savoy.* Running diagonally across the peninsula are the *Papal States.* In the south is the so-called Kingdom of the Two Sicilies, composed of *Naples* and *Sicily,* the former affording a bone of contention between France and Spain. (See **Hayes I,** 14-19; **Muir,** plates 8, 16, 17.)

Northern and Eastern Europe: Read **Hayes I** and study **Muir,** plate 8. Locate the states of the Union of Calmar. Note that *Finland* is still a part of Sweden. On the south and east of the Baltic are the lands *(Prussia, Kurland, Livonia, Esthonia)* of the Teutonic Knights. The overlord of these Teutonic Knights is the king of Poland, who rules over the united territories of *Poland* and *Lithuania,* one of the largest states in Europe. Has Poland any natural boundaries? To the east of this kingdom is the unimportant oriental state of *Russia.* To the east and north of the Habsburg territories are *Hungary* and its dependencies: *Bohemia, Moravia,* and *Silesia.*

Southern and Southeastern Europe: The threatening advance of the Ottoman Turks is the dominating fact in southern Europe. After the capture of *Constantinople* in 1453, the Turks rapidly overran the whole Balkan peninsula, including *Serbia, Bosnia, Bulgaria,* and *Wallachia.* Note (**Muir,** plate 1) how easily the Turks, controlling the highlands of the Balkans, can sweep down upon the Hungarian plain and threaten even Vienna. Under the greatest of the Ottoman rulers, Suleiman the Magnificent (1520-1566), the Turks will extend their dominions northward over this Hungarian plain. (In addition to the maps cited above, examine **Muir,** plate 25b.)

Map Study Number Two.

THE COMMERCIAL REVOLUTION.

Text: **Hayes I,** 27-28, 43-62. **Day,** 79-101.
Atlas: **Muir,** pp. 50-51; plates 46-49, 59-60. **D. R. Fox,** *Harper's Atlas of American History,* plates 1, 3-5. **D. S. Muzzey,** *American History,* p. 10.
McKinley Outline Map No. 100a.

It is the purpose of this study to illustrate that mighty expansive movement which broadened European history into world history, extending the influence of European civilization over all other continents and reacting powerfully to modify the economic life as well as the political ambitions of the European nations.

A. There is no better way to grasp the significance of the Commercial Revolution than comparing the "known world" before the great explorations of the fifteenth century with the world as we know it today. After consulting **Hayes I,** 27, 50, and **Muzzey,** 10, draw a red line encircling the portion of the earth's surface known to Europeans about the year 1400. Note by reference to **Muir,** plates 46-48, and **Fox,** 4, how slowly knowledge of world geography grew, even after the explorations of the Portuguese and Spanish.

B. **Trade before the Commercial Revolution:** The principal economic cause of the Commercial Revolution was the desire of the nations of Western Europe to share in the trade of the Orient by finding new routes to the land of spices, silks, and gold. These luxuries, introduced to the nobility of northern and western Europe by the Crusaders, had now come to be considered necessities. Read **Hayes I,** 44-45, and then indicate on the map the chief localities in which the commodities of Eastern trade were produced. A glance at **Muir,** 59-60, will show how medieval trade between Eastern Asia and Europe had to find its way through the few gaps in a great barrier-belt of deserts and mountain ranges. Indicate on your map a few of these physical obstacles to trade, such as the *Syrian Desert,* the barren tableland of *Arabia,* the *Hindu-Kush* Mountains. Observe how skilfully the medieval merchants, traveling the "old trade routes," avoided natural obstacles such as high mountain ranges and broad deserts. Consult **Hayes I,** 46-47, and map p. 49,

Muir, plates 59-60, **Fox,** 1; then trace by means of dotted lines (1) the route by which a packet of jewels would probably have been transported from India to England, in the fifteenth century, via the *"central route"*; (2) the route of a cargo of spices from the Moluccas to Stockholm via the *"southern route"*; (3) the route of a bale of silk from China to Novgorod. The interested student may compare the medieval trade routes with twentieth-century railway and steamship lines (**Shepherd,** 179-182).[1]

Note how the fortunate geographical situation of the Italian cities served to make them the hub of the trade with the East. Locate on your map four of the leading Italian commercial cities. Study the maps in **Day,** pp. 94, 106, 108, 114, to form an estimate of the importance of the German city-states and of certain cities of the Netherlands in medieval commerce. Locate on your map the cities mentioned in **Hayes I,** 49, and any trading centers of France and the Netherlands which you consider important. An explanation frequently advanced for the decline of these older towns after the Commercial Revolution is that their commerce with the Orient was strangled by Turkish occupation of the old trade-routes. Indicate the dates at which the old central and southern routes fell into the hands of the Ottoman Turks (**Hayes I,** 52-53) and compare with the dates of the successful explorations of the Portuguese. Does the result indicate that the Turkish conquests caused the Commercial Revolution? Do you think they accelerated it? (Consult also **Fox,** 2.)

C. **Exploration and Colonization:** From the year 1415, when an army of Portuguese crusaders (among whom was numbered the youthful Prince Henry the Navigator) conquered the Mohammedan stronghold of *Ceuta* in northern Morocco, expedition after expedition was sent out from Portugal to explore the seemingly interminable western coast of Africa. To mark the painfully slow progress of Portuguese exploration, indicate on your map *Madeira* (1419), *Cape Bojador* (1434), *Cape Blanco* (1440), *Cape Verde* (1445). (Consult, in addition to references already given, **Fox,** 4.) Trace the *voyage of Vasco da Gama* which finally crowned Portuguese perseverance with success. Meanwhile, Columbus, under the patronage of Queen Isabella, was striking out in exactly the opposite direction, hoping to reach the Indies by sailing westward. What Columbus hoped to accomplish and what he actually did accomplish

---

[1] Additional references to **W. R. Shepherd,** *Historical Atlas* (New edition, 1921), will be found on p. 160 below. Professor Shepherd's excellent atlas unfortunately was out of print when this syllabus went to press.

are indicated in **Muzzey,** 6, and **Fox,** 3; fix the voyages of Columbus clearly in your mind, but do not indicate them on your map. Note from **Muir,** plate 49b, that English and French explorers were seeking a "northwest passage" to the East.

Indicate on your map the important colonies of the European powers in the first quarter of the sixteenth century (consult **Muir,** plate 47, and **Fox,** 5). Were the Spanish colonies destined to be of assistance in the building up of trade with the Indies? What was to be their greatest importance?

Map Study Number Three

GROWTH OF THE HABSBURG POSSESSIONS, 1500-1598.

Text: **Hayes I,** 13, 74-106; **Muir,** pp. 9-10.
Atlas: **Muir,** plates 8, 15b, 25a; **Shepherd,** 118-119; **Hayes I,** map p. 3.
McKinley Outline Map No. 111a.

A. **Rise of the House of Habsburg:** By far the most powerful House in the Germanies in the sixteenth century was the Habsburg family. From small beginnings in the thirteenth century, their domain had grown to be the most important in Europe. In 1273 Rudolph, head of the Habsburg family, was elected ruler of the Empire as King of the Romans; by 1500 the title of Emperor had become practically hereditary in the family. Within a few generations after this Rudolph, the Habsburgs had secured Austria, Carinthia, Styria, Carniola, Tyrol (see Map Study No. 1) and small portions in the *Breisgau* and in *Alsace*. Just at the end of the fifteenth century their territories were greatly increased by the marriage of Maximilian I to Mary of Burgundy, daughter of Charles the Bold. During the sixteenth century the territory of the Habsburgs is still further augmented, and the family is destined to play the leading rôle in international, as well as in German politics.

B. **The Empire of Charles V:** Read very carefully **Hayes I,**

75-76, and **Muir**, pp. 9-10, in order to fix clearly in your mind the general development of the Habsburg empire. Now indicate on your map the lands inherited by Charles of Habsburg on the death of his father Philip, and of his grandfathers Maximilian of Austria and Ferdinand of Aragon. Mark off clearly the lands acquired by the Burgundian inheritance, and differentiate between the respective lands of the Spanish and Austrian legacies. (Consult **Muir**, references cited above.) Next show the lands acquired by the Habsburgs through the marriage of Ferdinand with Anne of Hungary. Over how much of Hungary did they make their claims effective?

Glance over your map and notice how scattered are these Habsburg territories. This makes graphic one of the great difficulties of the young Emperor,—the problem of administration over such a vast and diverse realm. This problem is the more complicated because each remote possession differed from the others in race, language, law, and custom. Name on your key sheet the various languages spoken by the subjects of Charles. It should be remembered, however, that these differences in race and language,—although they constituted practical difficulties in administration—were not serious obstacles in the maintenance of loyalty and obedience; the spirit of nationalism, so menacing a foe to the House of Habsburg in the nineteenth century, had not yet become of importance. Note, also, how the lands of Charles enclose the French kingdom; this fact will give point to many of the international enmities of the century.

C. **The division of the Habsburg inheritance:** After reading **Hayes I, 87**, show by shading or cross-hatching how Charles divided his territories in 1556.

Show European lands added to the Habsburg realm by Philip II (**Hayes I, 91**). This marks the apogee of Spanish Habsburg power. What lands were practically lost during Philip's reign? It should be remembered that his gains and losses involved not only European lands but important colonial possessions as well.

Map Study Number Four.

THE GROWTH OF FRANCE, 1500-1715.

Text: **Hayes I,** 209-218, 235-256; **Muir,** pp. 18-21.
Atlas: **Muir,** plates 1, 15; **Hayes I,** map p. 249.
McKinley Outline Map No. 124a.

The student should imagine himself in the place of the successive monarchs of France as they gradually created a well-rounded state; it will be advisable, therefore, to construct the map in chronological order. Select colors so that the earlier acquisitions will appear in darker, and the later acquisitions in lighter, tints.

We already have seen (Map Study Number One) that by the year 1500 the French kings had succeeded fairly well in consolidating their realm. Just at the close of the fifteenth century began a struggle with the Habsburgs which was to last for many generations, and for almost a hundred years the Valois kings of France were forced to fight hard to maintain intact their position and territories. The duchy of Milan, which the French held in 1500, changed hands several times only to be lost finally by the middle of the sixteenth century. A few gains the Valois dynasty did make: *Calais,* in 1559, was won at the expense of England; the important bishoprics of *Metz, Toul,* and *Verdun* were wrested from the Holy Roman Empire, although their French ownership was not recognized by the Emperor until almost a century later.

With the accession of the Bourbon family in the person of Henry of Navarre, France, urged on by the need of defensible frontiers and tempted by the weak condition of her neighbors, started on a career of aggression which was to raise her to the position of first state in Europe. In embarking upon the policy of "natural limits," Henry IV succeeded in forcing Savoy in 1601 to cede certain territories (including *Bresse* and *Bugey*) on the right bank of the Rhone in return for the marquisate of Saluzzo; by this exchange of territory France obtained an important "natural" and strategic frontier. In 1607 Henry declared the hereditary lands over which he ruled as king of Navarre to be united with France. These included *Navarre* and *Béarn* (although they were not finally incorporated until 1620), the counties of *Foix* and *Armagnac,* and the duchy of

Albret. (Consult for this section of the Study, **Muir**, plates 15b, 15c, 15d, and 17c.)

The extension of French frontiers eastward was notably advanced by the participation of France in the Thirty Years' War. After reading **Hayes I**, 228, and consulting **Muir**, plate 15c, show the territories secured by France under the terms of the Peace of Westphalia; note that certain of these were new acquisitions and others were earlier conquests the possession of which was now confirmed. Did these newly acquired territories serve to provide France with further "natural boundaries"? By the Peace of the Pyrenees, the southern border of France was carried to the crest of the Pyrenees; indicate the territories thus acquired.

Throughout the remainder of the seventeenth century, France, under her "Grand Monarch," Louis XIV, is to extend her frontiers to the north and east. After a careful reading of **Hayes I**, 242, 249, and a study of **Muir**, plate 15c, and **Hayes I**, map p. 249, show on your map the French gains secured by the various settlements from the peace of the Pyrenees to the peace of Ryswick (1697), indicating in your key sheet the treaties and the parties involved in each exchange of territory. Who are the chief losers through French aggrandizement? Observe the close connection of this study with the present-day question of Alsace-Lorraine. Note, too, England's interest in the maintenance of the integrity of the Netherlands,—an interest which becomes traditional in English foreign policy and is to provide the occasion for the entrance of Great Britain into the Great War of 1914-1918.

In his last great international conflict, the War of the Spanish Succession, Louis XIV was hard pressed to defend the frontiers which he already had acquired. The peace of Utrecht, however, is significant, for it meant: 1. That the fortunes of the two Bourbon powers, France and Spain, were to be closely linked for a century to come; 2. That France was to have a new and more powerful neighbor on the northeast by Austrian acquisition of the Netherlands; 3. That France, although she had fallen short of her desire for "natural boundaries," had emerged from two centuries of war with augmented territories and increased prestige.

While the French Bourbons were thus dearly purchasing a comparatively few square miles of the continent of Europe, they underestimated the fundamental importance of sea-power and overlooked opportunities for colonial and commercial aggrandizement. As we shall see, the mistake of France was the opportunity of Great Britain.

Map Study Number Five.

THE COLONIAL CONFLICTS OF FRANCE AND ENGLAND, 1688-1763.

Text: **Hayes I,** 299-319; **Fox,** *Harper's Atlas of American History,* 119-123, 134-139.

Atlas: **Hayes I,** 301, 317; **Muir,** plates 46-50, 53, 60-61; **Fox,** 5, 12, 13, 14, 16.

McKinley Outline Map No. 148a.

A. **The Europeanization of the World:** One of the great results of the explorations of the fifteenth and sixteenth centuries was the establishment of European empires throughout the world and the spread of European civilization to the four corners of the earth. The beginnings of that great expansive movement were considered in Map Study Number Two; it is the purpose of this Study to develop the theme through the seventeenth and eighteenth centuries. A thoughtful examination of **Muir,** plates 46-50, will show how quickly the European nations took advantage of the spread of geographical knowledge following the Commercial Revolution to plant their flags on continents unknown to them in 1400.

It will be noticed that the sixteenth century is a period of complete ascendancy of the Spanish and Portuguese in colonial affairs,— the Spanish endeavors being largely confined to Central America and the Portuguese to the East. The consolidation of the Spanish and Portuguese empires under Philip II (**Hayes I,** 91) is the high-water mark of Spanish colonial power. Note from **Muir,** plate 48, and from **Hayes I,** 58-59, how the Dutch, in the first half of the seventeenth century, successfully challenged Spanish ascendancy and carved out for themselves a colonial empire of no mean proportions. They carried their flag and their commerce to such widely separated points as the Spice Islands, the Malay Archipelago, Australia, Ceylon, India, Cape of Good Hope, Brazil, and New Netherlands. During this period of Dutch ascendancy the French and English tardily enter the field of colonial rivalries,—the French by establishing settlements along the St. Lawrence River and by beginning the exploration of the interior of North America; the English by the foundation of Virginia and New England and by the opening up of trade with India. Note, also, from **Muir,** plate 48, how geographical knowledge has increased throughout the sixteenth and seventeenth centuries; compare Drake's route in circumnavigating the globe with the earlier voyage of Magellan.

The latter part of the seventeenth and the beginning of the eighteenth century witness the systematic development of trade, exploration, and colonization by England and France in both the East and the West. This colonial activity is to lead to a world conflict between France and England for final ascendancy. In the meantime, the colonial empires of Spain, Portugal, and the Netherlands are either quiescent or on the decline. To make sure that you have clearly in mind the relative position of England and France in 1688, read **Hayes I,** 299-304 (with constant reference to appropriate plates in **Muir**); then in your key give a concise summary,— preferably in outline form—of the possessions of these rival powers in North America, in the West Indies, in India. What was to be the position of Spain and of the Netherlands in the coming struggle? (See **Hayes I,** 307-309, 311, 315).

B. **The colonial wars in America:** Without constructing a map of the colonial struggle in America, read **Fox,** Map Study entitled "Latin or Saxon? The Hundred Years' War," pp. 134-139, and refer to the plates there cited. What was the political and strategic importance of the Ohio Valley? Referring to **Hayes I,** 317-319, and **Fox,** 16, note on your key sheet the territorial changes in America registered by the peace of 1763. What American possessions were retained by France? What vestiges of French civilization still remain in North America?

C. **Anglo-French rivalry in India:** The conflict between France and England was decisive in at least one respect: henceforth India, an empire in itself, was to be English,—it might almost be said, the keystone of British imperialism. That a land the size and population of India should so easily fall prey to foreign domination is in itself a reason for query. After reading **Hayes I,** 302-303, and referring to **Muir,** plate 59, what reasons can you assign for the success of the English in controlling India? To gain some idea of the size of India, compare the distance between *Calcutta* and *Bombay* with that between London and Liverpool; between New York and Chicago; between Paris and Vienna. Why is it that India has not been made a field for colonization and conquest, as well as trade and tribute?

Indicate on the outline map the English and French trading posts established in the seventeenth century (**Hayes I,** 303-304) giving the date in each instance. Locate the lands of the Mogul Emperor at *Delhi.* His vassals and viceroys, by the eighteenth century practically independent princes, rule over such important territories as *Oudh, Bengal, Deccan* (capital at *Hyderabad*) and the *Carnatic.* Dupleix, the masterful French governor-general, extended French influence in the Carnatic from *Pondicherry* and consolidated the French position on the *Coromandel Coast;* he brought the *Northern Circars* under French control; he entered into the political intrigues of the native Indian rulers, in many cases enthroning puppets of his own, and in general increasing the prestige and power of France. To Robert Clive must be ascribed the credit of wrecking the grandiose schemes of Dupleix. Follow Clive's exploits on the map: his bold seizure and gallant defence of *Arcot* (1751); his recapture of *Calcutta* (1757); his conquest of *Chandernagore* (1757); his amazing victory of *Plassey* (1757). (Consult **Hayes I,** map p. 316; **Muir,** plate 61a.)

Although by the treaty of Paris (1763) France retained five unfortified posts in India, French political power in India was permanently destroyed. The British, however, pursued their imperial policy by intrigues with native princes and by the exercise of military ·force. Referring to **Muir,** plate 61a, and to **Hayes I,** map p. 316, indicate the extent of the British dominion and control at the end of the eighteenth century. Note from **Muir,** plate 61b, but do not indicate on your map, how British territory was still further increased by 1805.

Map Study Number Six.

THE GROWTH OF BRANDENBURG-PRUSSIA, 1415-1785.

Text: **Hayes I,** 347-362; **Muir,** p. 29.
Atlas: **Muir,** plate 24a; **Hayes I,** map p. 351, map p. 387; **Shepherd,** 122-123, 125.
McKinley Outline Map No. 125a.

Of the utmost importance in the history of modern Europe is the growth of Brandenburg-Prussia, under the rule of the House of Hohenzollern. A small, weak, unproductive state when the Hohenzollern prince, Frederick, secured it in 1415 at the hands of the Emperor Sigismund, it grew in territory, wealth, power, and prestige until, by the end of the eighteenth century, it had become a state of the first rank in Europe. In the nineteenth century it was destined to be of still greater importance: round it was to be knit together a united and powerful German Empire. The story of its growth is more simple .than that of Habsburg Austria, for it is a story of steady acquisition; the Hohenzollerns rarely relinquished territory once secured. Their story is one of power and triumph, occasionally interrupted but always resumed, until the Great War and a republican revolution forced their abdication and flight in 1918.

After reading **Hayes I,** 347-352, show the growth of the Hohenzollern lands from 1415 to the accession of Frederick II (1740). Indicate first, in solid color, the Mark of Brandenburg in the year 1415 (**Shepherd,** 85, or **Muir,** plate 24a). Then show the territories acquired from 1415 to 1608, without reference to the manner of acquisition. Next indicate additions made from 1608 to the accession of the Great Elector (1640). Observe how scattered the Hohenzollern territories are. To visit his Rhenish or Prussian possessions the Elector must cross neighboring and sometimes hostile lands. The one great aim of the rulers of Brandenburg-Prussia was to unite these scattered territories by securing the intervening lands. Trace now the additions made to the territory of Brandenburg under the various rulers from the Great Elector to the accession of Frederick II a century later, showing in your key when, from whom, and how each acquisition was made. (In this connection **Muir,** 24a, is inaccurate; a glance at **Shepherd,** 122-123, 125, will show that a strip of territory on the east bank of the Oder was not obtained until the treaty of St. Germain-en-Laye, 1679, a counterpart of the treaty of Nijmwegen.)

Show what accessions were made to Prussia as a result of the conflict between Frederick II (the Great) and Maria Theresa of Austria (read **Hayes I,** 354-362). What further extensions of territory were made during his reign? Show also what Prussia secured by the second and third partitions of Poland. (Consult **Muir,** plate 24a; **Hayes I,** map p. 351, map p. 387.)

Note that the territories of Prussia are now joined on the east. The Rhenish provinces are still detached, although several important connecting links have been forged; these western provinces will not be consolidated until almost a century later. Observe also that Prussia, long proud of her position as a purely German state in contrast with polyglot Austria, has acquired a considerable Slavic population through the partitions of Poland.

Map Study Number Seven.

THE FRENCH REVOLUTION AND THE ERA OF NAPOLEON.

Text: **Hayes I,** 449-519, 523-576; **Robertson,** p. 9; **Muir,** pp. 12-15.
Atlas: **Robertson,** plates 7-14; **Shepherd,** 134-135, 146-148, 150-157;
   Muir, plates 11, 12, 23d, 24b; **Hayes I,** maps pp. 479, 543, 559.
McKinley Outline Map No. 111a.

   A. **The Old Régime:** Draw in green the boundaries of France as they existed prior to the French Revolution (**Robertson,** plate 7). Note the acquisition of *Lorraine* in 1766 and of *Corsica* in 1768. Note that *Alsace* and Lorraine are still within the Holy Roman Empire (**Hayes I,** map p. 440) and subject to a network of imperial feudal rights and jurisdictions. This is only one example of confusing and overlapping divisions of administration in France. The first five maps in **Shepherd,** 146-148, are a graphic indictment of the old régime. Observe the administrative division of France into governments, judicial areas, and fiscal districts. Do these correspond even approximately in size and location? How order was brought out of this muddle by the Revolution will appear from **Hayes I,** 482-483, and the lower map in **Shepherd,** 148. Did the ecclesiastical divisions correspond to the administrative? (**Shepherd,** upper map 148.) Small wonder, then, that the philosophical reformers of the eighteenth century, seeking to reduce all human institutions to the rule of reason, should have condemned the old régime!
   B. **The Revolution:** Indicating the italicized places on the map (using numbers or initials explained in the key), review the progress of the French Revolution:—the assembling of the Estates

General at *Versailles;* the removal of the royal family and the Assembly to *Paris* in October, 1789; the attack upon the Church and the annexation of *Avignon;* the assembling of the émigrés at *Coblenz;* the fall of *Verdun;* the check at *Valmy;* the proclamation of the Republic; the anti-Jacobin risings in *Vendée, Gironde, Lyons, Marseilles,* etc. (In this section the student will find it advantageous to make liberal use of the indexes in **Muir** and **Shepherd.**)

The French Republic entered upon a career of military aggrandizement before the advent of Napoleon. This aggressiveness will help to explain the abhorrence with which conservatives after 1815 will regard all liberal or revolutionary movements. Color solidly green the lands annexed before Napoleon made himself master of France by the *coup d'état* of 1799 (**Hayes I,** map p. 479, map p. 559). Outline in yellow the dependent republics with which republican France surrounded herself (**Hayes I,** 516; **Shepherd,** 151).

C. **The Empire of Napoleon:** Napoleon continued the work of conquest, but created dependent monarchies instead of republics. The Ligurian Republic was annexed outright (1805); color it green. Outline in green the kingdoms of *Italy* (1805), *Naples* (1806), *Holland* (1806), *Westphalia* (1807), and *Spain* (1808), the grand-duchy of *Berg,* and the *Grand-Duchy of Warsaw,*—all under the effectual control of Napoleon. Now color in solid green the territory from the Rhine to *Lübeck,* annexed in 1810; the reason for this annexation will be clear if, remembering the Continental System, you place your pencil on Rotterdam, Amsterdam, Bremen, Hamburg, Lübeck. Italy, too, must be constrained to exclude British commerce; hence the annexation of certain of the Italian lands and of the *Illyrian Provinces,* all of which likewise should be colored green (see **Robertson,** plate 8). As more or less willing allies of Napoleon, enforcing the Continental System with varying degrees of vigor, *Austria-Hungary* (1809), *Sweden* (1810-1812), *Prussia* (1807), and *Denmark* may be outlined in blue. How much of the commercial coast of Europe now remains outside Napoleon's system? *Portugal,* backed by *Great Britain,* still defied the Emperor's will; color both red. Also *Sicily. Russia,* an ally in 1807, soon grew diffident and finally refused to enforce Napoleon's commercial decrees; outline Russia in red. The map now explains the underlying reason for the two wars which did most to undermine Napoleon's position,—the Peninsular War and the *invasion of Russia.* Indicate the latter by a dotted line. (See **Muir,** plate 11.)

D. **Consolidation in Germany:** In order to realize the complexity of "Germany" before the Napoleonic changes, turn to **Robertson,** plate 11, and attempt to count the states of the Holy Roman Empire in 1789. In 1806 Napoleon remade the map of Germany through the formation of the *Confederation of the Rhine.* Outline in green the Confederation as in 1812 (**Robertson,** plate 12; **Hayes I,** map p. 559; also **Muir,** p. 16), and note in your key the two important German states excluded from the Confederation. In thus remaking the map of Europe, Napoleon despoiled Prussia and Austria of much valuable territory. Indicate in your key some of the lands thus lost temporarily by those two states.

Although the Congress of Vienna was destined to restore Europe to its "legitimate" rulers, it will be evident from Map Study Number Eight that much of Napoleon's work will be permanent. This is particularly true of the Germanies, in which hundreds of petty principalities were destined to remain absorbed by a comparatively few larger states. But the Empire of Napoleon had an even greater permanent significance: it meant that the principles of the Revolution had been given practical application in many of the countries which were conquered by or allied with France. In this connection read once more **Hayes I,** 573-575.

Map Study Number Eight.

THE RECONSTRUCTION OF EUROPE BY THE CONGRESS OF VIENNA.

Text: **Hayes II,** 5-14; **Muir,** p. 15.
Atlas: **Robertson,** plates 13-17, 20-21; **Muir,** plates 12, 23d, 24b, 25a, 27; **Hayes II,** map p. 1.
McKinley Outline Map No. 101a (or Nos. 112a and 82a).

Refer back to Map Study Number Seven and to **Hayes I,** 558-566, and fix definitely in mind the political situation in Europe in 1813.

A. **Territorial adjustments in the interest of "legitimacy" and "compensations":** Draw the boundaries, as they existed in 1813, of the leading Continental allies leagued against Napoleon in the struggle of 1813-1814. After reading the text assignment, show the territories secured by each of these states by the settlement of Vienna. (It will be recalled that Russia already had acquired *Finland* and *Bessarabia*.) Point out in your key the most notable examples of "compensations." What had become of Napoleon's vassal states, such as, for example, the Grand-Duchy of Warsaw?

B. **The Germanic Confederation:** On the ruins of Napoleon's Confederation of the Rhine the Congress of Vienna constructed a Germanic Confederation, "a ghost of the old Holy Roman Empire." Draw the boundaries of the new Confederation. Note the consolidation and strengthening of the south German states; the readjustment of the western frontier, notably by large Prussian annexations of Rhenish territory; the protection which this extension of the frontier offers against French invasion of the Germanies; the reappearance of Hanover; the weakening of Saxony. Show on your map three or four free cities. Indicate territories within the Confederation but held by the kings of Denmark and the Netherlands. Show also Prussian and Austrian lands outside the Confederation. Locate on your map the free city of *Frankfort*, meeting place of the Diet of the Confederation.

C. **Violations of the principle of nationality:** In their enthusiasm for "legitimacy" and "compensations," the eminent statesmen at Vienna ignored the principle of nationalism. This fatal mistake was responsible for most of the wars of the nineteenth century,— it meant that, in spite of all Metternich might attempt for the maintenance of the *status quo,* the settlement of Vienna would not last. After reading **Hayes II,** 9-10, and **Muir,** p. 15, make clear on your map and explain in your key the important instances in which the Congress violated the principle of nationality.

Map Study Number Nine.

THE INDUSTRIAL REVOLUTION.

Text: **Hayes II,** 65-97; **Cheyney,** Chapter VIII; **H. de B. Gibbins,** *Industry in England* (New York, 1916), Chapters XX-XXV, may be consulted for special points.

Atlas: **Muir,** plates 30, 44a-b, and page 47; **Gibbins,** maps pp. 350 and 454; **Hayes II,** maps pp. 215 and 277.

Two McKinley Outline Maps No. 121a.

How the Industrial Revolution remade European society can be strikingly illustrated by comparing the England of, say, 1700, with the England of the nineteenth century,—when machinery and power had largely displaced hand labor, and the domestic system of manufacture had given way to the factory.

From **Muir,** plate 44b, indicate on your map in black oblique lines the chief coal-fields of England and Wales at the present time. With **Gibbins,** map p. 454, as a guide, show by red oblique lines the chief manufacturing districts of modern England; from **Muir,** 44b, make a mental note of the principal articles there manufactured. (These black and red oblique lines should be drawn as light as is consistent with clearness; if they are heavy, the colored portions of the map will become a blotch.) Tint lightly in green or yellow the districts most densely populated in present-day England. Observe to what extent the area of dense population corresponds with the area of manufacturing and mining. How can you account for the phenomenal growth of London and the district surrounding it?

The contrast between your map and one of England before the Industrial Revolution is striking. Compare your work with **Gibbins,** map p. 350, and **Muir,** plate 44a. On your key sheet enumerate the counties most densely populated before the Industrial Revolution; draw a red line through the names of those which no longer rank in the forefront; on the other hand, enumerate four counties which now are among the most densely populated, but which in 1750 were not. To explain this spectacular shift in population, observe that many of the declining counties were handicapped by lack of coal-fields or other industrial advantages. Referring to the physical map, **Muir,** plate 30, note how the rising counties possessed swift streams to furnish power for mills and mines.

It now remains to make graphic the effect of the Industrial Revolution upon British politics. On a second Outline Map No. 121a locate the following towns which were enfranchised in 1832: *Leeds, Sheffield* (where Sir Henry Bessemer proved the practical value of his method for the manufacture of steel), *Manchester* (center of the reform agitation up to 1832 and later of the Cobden-Bright free-trade movement), *Liverpool* (birthplace of William Ewart Gladstone), *Birmingham* (where Watt and Boulton manufactured steam engines), *Blackburn* (in the vicinity of which lived Hargreaves), *Bury* (home of John Kay, another of the inventors), *Rochdale* (in which was located the cotton mill of John Bright's father), *Sunderland* (famous for its coal exports as early as the reign of Henry VII). In each case, either on your map or in your key, indicate the branch of industry for which the town is famous; in some cases this information may be obtained from **Muir,** plate 44b, but in others it will be advisable to refer to articles on these towns in the *Encyclopædia Britannica.* Can you discover any correlation between these enfranchised towns and the shaded districts in your first map? Explain in your key.

Supplement to Map Study Number Nine.

A. **The British Cotton Industry.** The cotton industry was one of the first trades affected by the Industrial Revolution and may well be taken as an index. On a sheet of *cross-section paper* plot the growth of Great Britain's cotton industry, using the short way of the paper (each small space denoting five years) for the years, and the long way for the raw cotton imports (1 small space representing 30 millions of pounds). The following table from Mulhall's *Dictionary of Statistics* (p. 158) will give you the necessary data:

BRITISH IMPORTS OF RAW COTTON.

Year	Million Pounds
1720	2
1785	11
1800	52
1814	95
1820	119
1830	245
1840	452

Year	Million Pounds
1850	588
1860	1,140
1870	1,101
1880	1,404

At the proper places, chronologically, indicate on your graph-sheet the principal inventions which might have affected the cotton industry. Does the graph show a sudden rise after each invention? On the same sheet it may be worth while to show the increase of power-looms in the British cotton trade, using the following table:

Year	Looms
1813	2,400
1820	14,000
1829	55,500
1833	100,000
1870	440,000

B. The German Cotton Industry.

AVERAGE ANNUAL IMPORTS OF RAW COTTON

Years	Metric Tons
1836–1840	9,000
1856–1860	46,000
1876–1880	124,000
1886–1890	201,000
1899–1903	324,000

Compare with graph A. Was the Industrial Revolution in Germany synchronous with that in Great Britain?

C. The Russian Cotton Industry. To show the tardy development of modern industry in Russia, plot the graph of Russian imports of raw cotton, using the same scale as in A and B. Compare with Germany and Great Britain.

AVERAGE ANNUAL IMPORTS OF RAW COTTON.

Years	Tons
1824–1826	900
1836–1838	4,600
1842–1844	8,400
1848–1850	21,400
1889–1891	117,400
1899–1903	180,000

D. **The Iron Industry.** To show how the Industrial Revolution affected the iron industry, plot the growth of the British output of pig-iron. For purposes of comparison the interested student may also indicate (preferably in ink or pencil of another color) the growth of the French, German, American, and World output.

ESTIMATED AVERAGE ANNUAL OUTPUT OF PIG-IRON,
IN THOUSAND TONS.

Date	Great Britain	France	United States	Germany	Total World
1500	6	12	......	5	60
1700	12	22	......	10	104
1740	20	26	1	18	157
1750	22				
1790	68	40	30	30	278
1800	190	60	40	40	460
1810	250	85	55	45	616
1820	400	140	110	90	1,010
1830	680	220	165	120	1,585
1840	1,400	350	290	170	2,680
1850	2,250	570	560	400	4,442
1860	3,830	900	820	530	7,180
1870	5,960	1,180	1,670	1,370	11,910
1880	7,750	1,730	3,840	2,700	18,140
1890	7,900	....	9,200	4,580	27,160
1900	8,960	....	13,790	8,390	38,970

(From Mulhall, *Dictionary of Statistics*, p. 332, and *Enc. Brit.*, vol. XIV, p. 834.)

Similar graphs may be constructed to illustrate the relationship between the Industrial Revolution and the development of international commerce, the growth of population in the various European countries, and other relevant phenomena. For such purposes the interested student or instructor will find statistical material available in Mulhall, *Dictionary of Statistics;* Webb, *New Dictionary of Statistics;* the *Encyclopædia Britannica.*

Map Study Number Ten.

THE UNIFICATION OF ITALY, 1848-1871.

Text: **Hayes II,** 163-175.
Atlas: **Muir,** plate 18b; **Robertson,** plates 16-17; **Hayes II,** maps
pp. 165 and 427.
McKinley Outline Map No. 132a.

Recall the reorganization of the Italian peninsula accomplished by
Napoleon (see Map Study Number Seven) and the virtual undoing
of his work by the Congress of Vienna (see Map Study Number
Eight). Although by the terms of that settlement the House of
Habsburg tightened its grip more firmly than ever upon Italy, the
Kingdom of Sardinia emerged with increased territory acquired
at the expense of Genoa. Recall also the unsuccessful attempt of
Sardinia to drive Austria from Italian soil in 1848 (**Hayes II, 131,**
136-137). By this defeat success was not permanently denied, but
only postponed.

As you read the text assignment, try to visualize the growth of
a united Italy by constant reference to the atlas. Draw on your
outline map the Kingdom of Sardinia as it was in 1848. Indicate
the territories which Cavour promised to Napoleon III as the
price of French aid against Austria. Now trace on your map the
steps in the unification of Italy, indicating in your key when and
how each state was annexed to Sardinia (1859-1860). Then show
what the newly constituted Kingdom of Italy secured from the
alliance of 1866 with Prussia. Indicate what additional steps toward
unification were taken during the Franco-German War of 1870-
1871.

Had Italy now reached her national boundaries? Show on your
map those lands of Italian speech which still remained in the possession of the Habsburgs. This *Italia irredenta* will serve as the
chief explanation of the entrance of Italy into the Great War
(1915). (See **Hayes II, p. 427.**)

Map Study Number Eleven.

THE FOUNDATION OF THE GERMAN EMPIRE,
1815-1871.

Text: **Hayes II,** 180-202.
Atlas: **Muir,** plates 23d, 24b, 12-13, 51d; **Robertson,** plates 13-14;
    Hayes II, map p. 181, map p. 211.
McKinley Outline Map No. 125a.

Refer back to Map Study Number Eight to review the political situation in the Germanies after the Congress of Vienna. On your new outline map draw the boundaries of Prussia as they were determined in 1815. This Prussian state will gain considerably in size and prestige until, in 1871, it will be the leading state of the Germanies and the keystone of a new and powerful German Empire.

The political unification of Germany was preceded by an economic union of the principal German states. Show, by a blue line, the boundaries of this Zollverein, or customs union, in 1834. And now the states which subsequently joined, indicating the date in each instance. Explain in your key what influence this economic union would be likely to exert in the direction of political union. Observe that Austria, which consistently has opposed a strong unified state, is not included in this economic union.

Following carefully **Hayes II,** 186-191, indicate by oblique lines the various acquisitions to Prussian territory as a result of the wars with Denmark and Austria (1864-1866), enumerating in your key the states thus annexed. Among these annexed territories locate *Kiel,* which subsequently was to be the eastern terminus of an important naval and commercial canal connecting the North Sea with the Baltic. Note that the Prussian state now is thoroughly consolidated,—east and west are finally joined. Observe also that Prussia has gained control of an attractive stretch of seacoast with strategic harbors; this is destined to make the new German Empire a great commercial, colonial, and naval power.

Draw the boundaries of the North German Confederation (1867-1871) and color the non-Prussian states of the Confederation to distinguish them from Prussian territory. Indicate in your key the German states which remained outside this new Confederation.

Show on your map, with appropriate explanations in your key, the results of the Franco-German War (1870-1871) in the final achievement of German unification. Indicate clearly the portions of Alsace and Lorraine ceded by France to the German Empire. These ceded territories included several strong fortresses and valuable iron mines, thus giving them increased political and economic importance.

The German Empire, welded together by "iron and blood," was undoubtedly firmly united, prosperous, and powerful; but it was not coterminous with the German nation. Millions of Germans still remained outside the German national state. After consulting **Hayes II**, pp. 427 and 435, describe in your key the territorial distribution and political allegiance of these German-speaking peoples. Furthermore, in achieving "national unification" for themselves the Germans had violated the principle of nationalism by including within the Empire considerable numbers of non-German peoples. To the Polish problem in *Posen* had been added a Danish problem in *Schleswig* and a French problem in *Alsace-Lorraine*. These racial minorities will constitute a political weakness of the German Empire until they are finally set free by the Peace of Versailles in 1919.

Map Study Number Twelve.

THE NEAR EASTERN QUESTION.

Text: **Hayes II**, 422, 426-435, 468-469, 490-539, 706-707.
Atlas: **Robertson**, plates 3, 18-26, 29-30; **Muir**, 26a; **Hayes II**, maps pp. 331, 427, 491, 535; **Hayes III**, maps pp. 128, 138.
McKinley Outline Map No. 113a.

A. **The Dismemberment of the Ottoman Empire:** After referring to **Hayes II**, map p. 491, and **Muir**, plate 26a, draw a line indicating approximately the greatest extent of the Ottoman Empire. Then draw a second line bounding the Empire in 1815 (**Hayes II**, map p. 1). Third, draw a line showing the Turkish frontiers of 1914 (**Hayes II**, maps pp. 535, 561). These lines show that the map of southeastern Europe was altered more radically in the single century 1815-1914 than in all the preceding three hundred years.

Fix clearly in your mind, but do not indicate on your map, the losses of the Ottoman Empire which were due to the emancipation of Magyar and Ruman territory by the Austrian Habsburgs; the apparently irresistible advance of the Russians along the Black Sea and in the Caucasus; imperialistic aggrandizement of France, Great Britain, and Italy in the African, Mediterranean, and Asiatic provinces of the Sultan. It will be advisable to describe in your key these gains of the various European nations at the expense of the Turks.

The most significant development of the nineteenth and twentieth centuries in the dismemberment of the Ottoman Empire, however, is the struggle of the Balkan peoples to throw off the yoke of Turkish rule. In this struggle geography was on the side of the Christian peoples struggling for their independence; glance at **Muir**, plate 28a, and see how well-nigh impossible it was for the Turks to bring under subjection by military force the tribesmen of Serbia, Montenegro, Albania, and Bulgaria. The goal of national independence from Turkey was practically achieved by the Balkan Wars of 1912-1913; show on your map, therefore, the Balkan States as their boundaries were defined by the Treaty of Bucharest (**Hayes II**, map p. 535). As we shall see presently, however, the final achievement of national unification for these nations could be realized only after a struggle against the Habsburgs; this fact will explain the stakes of Austria-Hungary in the Balkans and the rôle of the Balkan nations in the Great War. The Treaty of Bucharest was not a peace, but only a truce.

B. **Austro-Hungarian Ambitions in the Balkans:** The forcible expulsion of Austria from Italy and from participation in German affairs (see Map Studies Numbers Ten and Eleven) led the Habsburgs to seek new fields for dynastic and imperial aggrandizement. Following the course of least resistance, they initiated a *Drang nach Osten* designed, ultimately, to bring the entire Balkan Peninsula under their control. To their Serbo-Croat provinces of *Croatia, Slavonia,* and *Dalmatia,* they added by annexation (1909) the provinces of *Bosnia* and *Herzegovina.* Thus was forecasted the southward expansion of Austria-Hungary which was not to be definitely halted until crushing military defeats and a republican revolution in 1918 brought about the disintegration of the empire of the Habsburgs.

In a sense, Austro-Hungarian policy in the Balkans was defensive. The avowed purpose of certain of the Balkan states to achieve full national unification constituted a threat to Austria-Hungary that one day she would be obliged to surrender some of her most important territories. Referring to **Robertson,** plate 18, and to **Hayes II,** map p. 427, indicate in your key those provinces of Austria-Hungary which would have to be given up if the "Greater Serbia" was to be realized. It was charged in 1914 that the Serbian government was countenancing nationalist agitation by Serbians for the forcible seizure of these provinces and for the fomenting of local insurrections. Locate *Serajevo,* the scene of the murder which provided the occasion for the Great War in 1914. Observe, also, that a "Greater Rumania" would involve for Austria-Hungary the loss of such valuable provinces as *Transylvania* and *Bukowina.* Only if the Habsburgs maintained control of the Balkan states could they hope to stave off eventual disintegration of their empire.

These conflicting nationalist aims were complicated by the desire of Austrian and Hungarian capitalists to control the Balkan railways. Draw the line of the railway which connects Vienna with Constantinople, via Budapest, *Belgrade, Nish, Sofia,* and *Adrianople.* Show the off-shoots of this railway terminating in *Salonica,* the important Greek port on the Ægean. Note that Serbian acquisition of the sanjak of *Novi Bazar* during the Balkan Wars deprived Austria of the possibility of acquiring another natural railway route to Salonica. The economic and strategic importance of these railways provided one of the chief incentives to an aggressive Austrian policy in the Near East. To gain possession of these routes was the main purpose of the Austro-German conquest of Serbia in 1915. (See **Hayes II,** map p. 535, and **Hayes III,** map p. 128).

C. **The Stakes of Germany in the Near East:** The Balkan policy of Austria-Hungary was responsible for a number of Near Eastern crises (see **Hayes II,** 706-709) which brought Europe many times to the brink of war and which, in 1914, resulted in the precipitation of the greatest international struggle of all time. That Germany, in each of these crises, faithfully stood beside her ally "in shining armor" will the more readily be understood if one expresses in graphic form the coincidence of German and Austro-Hungarian interests in the Near East.

German imperialism in the Near East centered in the Bagdad Railway. This railway, it was hoped, eventually would provide through service from Berlin to the Persian Gulf and thence by steamer to India. In Europe the line would run from Berlin to

Constantinople via Vienna, Budapest, and the main Balkan railway mentioned above. Thus far, then, Germany would be vitally interested in the maintenance of Austrian hegemony in the Balkan Peninsula. After consulting **Hayes III**, map p. 138, draw the line of the Bagdad Railway in Asiatic Turkey: the route will lead you from *Scutari* through *Aleppo* and *Mosul* to *Bagdad, Basra,* and *Koweit* (See, also, **Robertson**, plate 26). Note that at Aleppo connections are made for *Damascus,* Jerusalem, and Mecca, bringing the line perilously near the *Suez Canal.* Observe the proposed branch lines in Persia. (Note throughout this section that only portions of the Bagdad Railway have been actually completed.)

Glance over **Hayes II**, map p. 561, and fix clearly in your mind the colonies and spheres of interest of the European nations in Asia. Does an examination of your map of the Bagdad Railway suggest anything as to the reasons for British opposition to the project? Why should Russia have objected to the Railway? Explain in your key sheet. The Great War was destined to transfer the Bagdad Railway to British hands.

Map Study Number Thirteen.

INTERNATIONAL RELATIONS AND THE GREAT WAR.

Text: **Hayes II**, 679-719; **Hayes III**, 13-27, 37-40, 62-65, 69-73.
Atlas: **Robertson**, plates 1, 4, 6, 9, 10, 13, 17; **Hayes II**, maps pp. 331, 397, 427; **Hayes III**, maps pp. 1, 27, 143, 299, 327; *Hammond's Business Atlas of Economic Geography,* plates 10-11.
McKinley Outline Map No. 111a.

The student is advised to examine all of the atlas material before beginning this Study; otherwise he will have some difficulty in locating readily the information required.

A. **France and Germany:** European and world politics are so intimately associated with the sharp rivalry between France and Germany that a clear understanding of their relations to each other is the first necessary step in a study of the international relations of the latter nineteenth and early twentieth centuries. Draw the boundaries of France and of the German Empire as they were in 1914. Refer to *Hammond's Business Atlas of Economic Geography*, plates 10-11, and indicate on your map the chief coal fields and iron mines near the Franco-German border and in Belgium. Of no inconsiderable importance are the valuable iron ore deposits in Lorraine, partly in French and partly in German territory. Note from **Robertson,** plate 4, how exposed to attack from either side are the industrial districts of France, Belgium, and the Rhenish provinces of Prussia; whoever possesses these will be depriving his enemy of the very sinews of war. Observe the situation of *Alsace-Lorraine* with reference to the "natural boundaries" of France and to the ethnographical limits of the French-speaking peoples. Color France solid green; Germany solid yellow; Great Britain with red oblique lines.

B. **The Balance of Power:** Outline in yellow the Triple Alliance by which Bismarck effected the diplomatic isolation of France and maintained German hegemony in European affairs until he retired as Chancellor (1890). In the years following 1890 France was determined to recover from this humiliating isolation and to build up a rival coalition to offset the prestige and power of the Central European alliance. The first step in the successful pursuit of this policy was the cementing of the Dual Alliance between France and Russia (1891-1895); color Russia with green oblique lines. Great Britain, still neutral, was inclined to be anti-French because of conflicting colonial policies; one of these clashes nearly precipitated a war between the two countries in 1898 (Refer to **Hayes II,** 624, and explain in your key). Largely through the masterly diplomacy of Delcassé, the negotiations succeeding the incident of 1898 resulted in the formation of the Entente Cordiale of 1904; green cross-lines should now be drawn over Great Britain. Divergent interests in the Near East and the Far East at first prevented any agreement between the two allies of France, Russia and Great Britain; these were reconciled by agreements of 1907, completing the Triple Entente; Russia should now be colored with red cross-lines. Japan, if on the outline map, likewise would be colored with cross-hatching of green and red (explain in your key). Portugal may be outlined in red, as an ancient ally of Great Britain.

In the face of this seemingly hostile coalition, Germany desired to cement her existing alliance and, perhaps, to enlist the aid of new friends. She loyally supported Austro-Hungarian policy in the

Balkans, thus increasing German prestige in Vienna. Russian influence became predominant in Serbia after 1903 (explain in your key); outline Serbia in green and red to indicate allegiance to the policies of the Entente. Thereafter the Teutonic powers tended to favor Bulgaria (outline brown) rather than Serbia. German economic penetration into Turkey was winning the political support of the Sultan; outline Turkey in brown. Meanwhile Italy was becoming restive in the Triple Alliance; she was suspicious and jealous of the Balkan policy of Austria-Hungary; she still cast longing, envious glances toward *Italia irredenta*. To show the growth of pro-Entente feeling in Italy, scatter a few green dots over the peninsula.

Your map should now give you a graphic picture of the diplomatic situation in Europe when the assassin of Serajevo fired a shot which shook the world.

C. **The Great War:** Obviously no single map study could give an adequate picture of the Great War; it will be necessary for us to confine our attention to a few significant developments of the momentous years 1914-1918.

Following closely the Topical Outline (pp. 95-103 above), with appropriate references to **Hayes III,** color with green and yellow oblique lines respectively the nations of Europe which entered the war associated with the Entente or the Teutonic powers. (It will be found helpful in this connection to consult **Hayes III,** maps pp. 143 and 299.) In your key name the non-European nations which entered the war against Germany.

Refer to **Hayes III,** maps pp. 27 and 327, and then show on your map approximately the portions of Belgium and northern France devastated by the war. How far does this area coincide with the industrial and mining districts which you already have indicated on your map? Now read **Hayes III,** 21-27, 37-40. What reasons do you think prompted the Germans to invade France via Belgium, rather than via Lorraine? Explain in your key.

Supplement to Map Study Number Thirteen.

While it is necessary to have a vivid mental picture of the geographical situation of the European nations and of their international alliances, it is hardly less desirable to form a clear conception of their relative importance in population, industry, and trade. Statistics are easily accessible in encyclopædias, the *Statesman's Year Book,* and the *World Almanac.* The student should compile from these sources a table of the populations of the chief European nations. On a graph sheet, turned so that the longer side of the sheet is horizontal, he should write the names of the countries at the left-hand margin, one under the other in a vertical column, leaving about an inch space at the top. Opposite each name should be inked in a heavy line proportioned in length to the population of the country, allowing each small space to represent, say, 5,000,000. Population is here taken merely as an example of how the graph may be constructed. Similar procedure may be followed, at the option of the student, to show relative strength of the belligerent nations in commerce, cotton manufactures, iron and steel production, wheat production, armies, navies, colonial empires.

Map Study Number Fourteen.

EUROPE IN 1920.

Text: **Hayes III,** 365-388.
Atlas: *Statesman's Year Book,* 1919 and 1920; **Hayes II,** maps pp. 331 and 701; **Hayes III,** maps pp. 365, 374, 375, 401.
McKinley Outline Maps Nos. 112a, 114b, 113a.

A. **The New Map of Germany:** On outline map No. 112a show German territory occupied by the Allies under the terms of the armistice of November 11, 1918 (*Statesman's Year Book,* 1919, and **Hayes III,** map p. 358). Now, using *Statesman's Year Book,* 1919, and **Hayes III,** maps pp. 365, 374, 375, show how the map of Germany was remade by the Treaty of Versailles. Indicate what areas were to have their nationality determined by plébiscite. Explain in your key the status of the Saar Valley.

B. **The New National States:** One of the remarkable developments of the Great War was the disintegration of the empires of Russia and Austria-Hungary and the breaking away of racial minorities throughout Europe from their former oppressors. The settlement of 1919 attempted to recognize the principle of nationality; and wherever racial minorities were not given complete independence, to protect their rights from infringement by the majority. Now, using all three outline maps according as they seem to you most convenient for each purpose, show how the principle of nationality was intended to be vindicated by certain annexations of the Allied Powers, notably France and Italy. Far more important than these annexations, however, was the creation of new national states. Show on your maps the Republic of *Poland;* the Republic of *Czechoslovakia;* the Baltic republics of *Finland, Esthonia, Latvia, Lithuania,* and the free city of *Danzig;* the Republic of *Hungary;* the *Ukrainian Republic;* the Kingdom of *Jugoslavia* (Kingdom of the Serbs, Croats, and Slovenes); and any others of importance. Compare your map as now constituted with **Hayes II,** map p. 331. How far has the principle of nationality been incorporated in the settlement? Is the Peace of 1919 more successful in this respect than was the Peace of Vienna? Can you discover any violations of the principle of nationality? (Answer these questions in your key.)

C. **The Dismemberment of Turkey:** The best reference for this section is the *Statesman's Year Book,* 1920. The Treaty of Sèvres effectually destroyed the last vestiges of the once great empire of Suleiman the Magnificent and his successors. The "Sick Man" of Europe at last passed away. Indicate the disposition of Turkish territory in Europe. What solution was arrived at in the delicate question of *Constantinople* and the *Straits?* Show on your map applications of the principle of mandates in the cases of *Smyrna, Palestine, Mesopotamia,* and *Syria,* indicating in each instance the name of the mandatary power. The principle of nationality again was vindicated in the recognition of the independence of the Republic of *Armenia,* of the Transcaucasian republics of *Georgia* and *Azerbaijan,* and of the Kingdom of the *Hedjaz.*

D. **Disposition of the German Colonial Empire:** Compare **Hayes II,** map p. 701, with **Hayes III,** map p. 401. Explain in your key which nation obtained the lion's share of the spoils in the Allied partition of the colonial empire of Germany. What disposition was made of the German lease of Kiao-chao and other concessions in the Chinese province of Shantung? What was the attitude of the Chinese Republic toward this settlement? (Explain in your key.)

ADDITIONAL ATLAS MATERIAL

The attention of the student is called to the following additional references in **Shepherd** (New edition, 1921) and in F. J. C. Hearnshaw, *Macmillan's Historical Atlas of Modern Europe* (London, 1920).

Map Study Number One: *Physical,* **Shepherd,** 2, 62, 91; *Political,* for England, **Shepherd,** 74, 84, 118; for France, **Shepherd,** 81, 85; for the Iberian Peninsula, **Shepherd,** 83, 118; for the Germanies, **Shepherd,** 86, 114; for Italy, **Shepherd,** 90, 118; for other countries, **Shepherd,** 2, 113-119, 124.

Map Study Number Two: *Part B,* **Shepherd,** 2, 98, 102, 179, 182; *Part C,* **Shepherd,** 107-110, 174.

Map Study Number Three: **Shepherd,** 86, 114, 118.

Map Study Number Four: **Shepherd,** 126; **Hearnshaw,** 2.

Map Study Number Five: *Part A,* **Shepherd,** 107-110, 112, 128; *Part C,* **Shepherd,** 128, 132, 137.

Map Study Number Six: **Shepherd,** 85, 87, 115, 121-123, 125, 133-135, 138; **Hearnshaw,** 5, 7.

Map Study Number Seven: *Part A,* **Shepherd,** 134, 146-149; *Part B,* **Shepherd,** 146-149, 150; *Part C,* **Shepherd,** 150-157; *Part D,* **Shepherd,** 152, 155, 157.

Map Study Number Eight: **Shepherd,** 142, 157-159.

Map Study Number Nine: **Shepherd,** 162-163.

Map Study Number Ten: **Shepherd,** 161; **Hearnshaw,** 13.

Map Study Number Eleven: **Shepherd,** 157, 158, 160; **Hearnshaw,** 9.

Map Study Number Twelve: **Hearnshaw,** 11, 15.

Map Study Number Fourteen: **Hearnshaw,** plate 11, pp. 21-23.

Appendix III.

BOOK REVIEWS.

A useful exercise in the study of modern history is the preparation of a paper on some historical book. Such a "review" is expected to achieve two quite different ends—the one, informational; the other, critical. As a means of acquainting himself with the methods of competent writers, the student should read one or more typical book reviews in *The Nation* (New York), *The American Historical Review, Political Science Quarterly,* or some similar publication.

Information Concerning the Book Reviewed.

At the beginning of every review should be written with accuracy the title, author, publisher, date, pagination, etc., of the book under consideration. For example, the review should be prefaced by such a heading: *The British Empire and the United States.* By William Archibald Dunning. With an introduction by Viscount Bryce and a preface by Nicholas Murray Butler. New York, Charles Scribner's Sons, 1914: xl, 381 pp. Then the reviewer should set forth succinctly the plan and scope of the work, rehearse clearly the main ideas developed, and report carefully the kind of sources and method which the author appears to have used. The seeming formality of such a summary should not dissuade the reviewer from using whatever art he may possess, as an intelligible summary requires not only insight in discerning what is of primary importance and what is merely explanatory and dependent, but also a considerable amount of sympathy and a facility to express in a few written pages the substance of a volume. It is hoped that by this practice the student will himself learn to read more intelligently.

Criticism of the Book Reviewed.

The student should ascertain from the introduction or preface, or by reference to some biographical dictionary such as *Who's Who,* something of the author's training, occupation, previous writings, and political and religious affiliations. This information is important in determining the writer's qualifications and in explaining his prejudices, should he have any.

As a reviewer the student must now summon his faculties of criticism wisely to evaluate what he has considered and described. He has indicated in general the author's purpose; it is now his function to sit in judgment to decide in how far that purpose has been realized. Does the book tell you what you wish to know about the subject? Does the author's style attract or repel the reader? Does he seem fair in his interpretation of evidence or do his judgments seem unwarranted by the facts he cites? Why, if at all, should anyone pay money for this book and spend time in reading it? Does it succeed as well as other books you know upon this or similar subjects? Considering the many things that men and women have to do, is it wise to foster interest in such subjects? To whom would you recommend such reading, and why? These are not questions which can be answered without thought; and in thus measuring the book in the larger terms of human experience the review will gain a value of its own. It is hoped that by this practice the student will himself learn to develop his critical faculties.

There is no need, of course, in such a piece of writing for the reviewer to draw a hard and fast line between information and criticism, putting into part one what the book says and into part two what is said about it. Rather, as a rule, the two will go side by side to attract or warn the general reading public for whom, it is supposed, the review is prepared.

[Adapted from instructions in *A Syllabus of American History and Map Studies* by Robert Livingston Schuyler and Dixon Ryan Fox.]

Appendix IV.

HISTORICAL ESSAYS.

No fundamental course in history is complete unless it provides the student with instruction and practice in the methods of historical research and in the preparation of suitable essays based upon this research. The purpose of such essay work is to train the student in three fundamental things:

1. The preparation of a bibliography,—that is, investigation to ascertain the best books, magazine articles, and other writings upon a particular topic.

2. The taking of notes in correct form, based upon several of the best and most accessible works dealing with the subject.

3. The construction, from the information thus acquired, of an essay conforming to accepted principles of historical composition.

The task here outlined will involve intelligent use of the facilities of the library, as well as critical evaluation and selection of material, —useful exercises in themselves.

Selection of a Subject.

The first step in the selection of a subject is the choice of a general historical field in which the essay is to be written; such a choice might be the French Revolution, the Era of Napoleon, the Era of Metternich, the Industrial Revolution, the Great War. Within the general field thus elected, the student now should decide upon a particular topic or subject, such as, The Reign of Terror; Napoleon and the Bank of France; Metternich and the Suppression of Liberalism in the Germanies; The Effect of the Industrial Revolution on the English Laboring Classes; The Republican Revolution of 1918 in Germany. The final choice of a subject should be made at an individual conference between the student and his instructor.

Preparation of Bibliography.

As soon as the student receives his assignment he will make a list of all major works bearing upon his topic. He should secure probably thirty or forty titles of books or magazine-articles. Each such title should be entered clearly in ink upon a separate card, together with the name of the author, the date of publication, and, wherever possible, the Library call number, the bibliographer's estimate of the work (if any), and some indication of the portion of it dealing most directly with the student's topic. It is expected that the student will be at pains to learn all that he can, in a general way, about the books cited, so as to talk intelligently about them in conference. And the student who has any sort of reading knowledge of French, German, Italian, or Spanish, should not hesitate to include in his bibliography titles of books in foreign languages which he understands, for some of the best work on the history of modern Europe has been written in foreign languages and is not translated into English.

To secure titles of books bearing upon his topic the student will consult the appropriate chapter-bibliographies in the text-book; in J. H. Robinson and C. A. Beard, *Readings in Modern European History*, Vol. I, pp. 389-410, and Vol. II, pp. 521-541; and, for nineteenth-century subjects exclusively, in C. D. Hazen, *Europe since 1815* (1910), pp. 737-772. Moreover, the *Cambridge Modern History*, a standard work in twelve volumes, contains at the end of each volume long book lists, though unfortunately without descriptive comment: Vol. VI deals with the eighteenth century; Vol. VII, the United States; Vol. VIII, the French Revolution; Vol. IX, Napoleon; Vol. X, 1815-1848; Vol. XI, 1848-1870; Vol. XII, 1870-1900. There are likewise useful bibliographies at the end of many articles in the standard encyclopedias, notably in the *Encyclopædia Britannica*, 11th ed., 29 vols. (1910-1911), in the *New International Encyclopædia*, 2d ed., 24 vols. (1914-1916), and in the *Catholic Encyclopædia*, 15 vols. (1907-1912): in using an encyclopedia, the student should remember to look in the index for topics related to his own. If his topic is in English history, the student should also consult the *Dictionary of National Biography*, 72 vols. (1885-1913), under the alphabetically arranged names of the principal persons important in relation to his subject; and H. L. Cannon, *Reading References for English History*. If his topic is in German history and he reads German, the student should consult Dahlmann-Waitz, *Quellenkunde der deutschen Geschichte*, 8th ed. (1912). If the student reads French, he should consult the bibliographies at the close of the appropriate chapters in the *Histoire générale du IVe siècle à nos jours*, ed. by Ernest Lavisse and Alfred Rambaud, 12 vols. (1894-1901): Vol. VII treats of the eighteenth century; Vol. VIII, French

Revolution; Vol. IX, Napoleon; Vol. X, 1815-1847; Vol. XI, 1848-1870; Vol. XII, 1870-1900.

To secure titles of magazine-articles bearing upon his topic the student should consult *Poole's Index* (1802-1906) and *Readers' Guide* (1900-   ). Pertinent newspaper comment may be located by reference to the *New York Times Index* and the *Times Index* (London).

Having completed his list of books and magazine-articles in manner as just set forth, the student will ascertain, by consulting the catalogue in the library, what ones are readily obtainable, and, having indicated the library call-numbers on the respective cards for such books, he will then submit his bibliography to the instructor, again in personal consultation, for discussion and criticism. At this second consultation, the instructor will assign a few of the more important books and articles, and these are to be read by the student and used as a basis for note-taking.

Preparation of Notes.

Notes, based upon careful reading of the works assigned, should now be taken in a neat, orderly manner. Preferably they should be written upon cards or papers of about 5½ by 8½ inches, running lengthwise of the page, liberal margins being left at the sides for page references or other comment. At the top of each such card or paper an entry should be made describing the general nature of the notes thereon and indicating the sources of information from which they have been derived. A completed card would look something like this:

Economic development of   Gibbons, *New Map of*
Germany after War of 1870   *Europe,* pp. 38-39.

Greatest era of industrial growth and prosperity ever known in history of world,—surpassing even that of United States. Growth of cities. Railway construction, "a network of steel." Mines and factories. Increase in population. Growth of merchant marine. Desire for foreign markets. Etc., etc.

A note thus taken may be a summary, or it may be a quotation, or it may be a combination of these. After sufficient material has been gathered for the essay, the student should arrange his notes in the order which he expects to follow in writing his essay. He may supplement his notes, if he so desire, with a brief topical outline or other plan for his paper. Notes and plan should be submitted to the instructor for criticism and for advice concerning the composition of the essay.

Composition of the Essay.

The essay should follow the accepted principles of English composition. It should scrupulously avoid the inclusion of irrelevant material; it should be coherent; it should be written in clear idiomatic English and the best literary style of which the student is capable. In general, the essay should follow the notes but should not follow them so closely as to limit the imagination or individuality of the student. Should it be advisable to use the exact words of a book or article, quotation marks should indicate the precise extent of the direct quotation. Thus will the essay demonstrate the student's ability to select, digest, and edit information derived from a number of sources.

Historically, the essay must be strictly and scrupulously accurate. *Every important statement of fact should be substantiated by a footnote or marginal note citing the authority for that statement* (including title of book and page reference). The student should submit his complete work (bibliography, notes, and essay) for rating and criticism as a whole.

Every manuscript should be as carefully prepared as if it were intended for the hands of the printer. Therefore, the essay should be neatly typewritten or carefully and legibly written in ink, on one side only of large-size paper.